EDITOR: MARTIN WINDROW

MEN-AT-ARMS SERIES 116

OSPREY MILITARY

THE SPECIAL AIR SERVICE

Text by
JAMES G SHORTT
Colour plates by
ANGUS McBRIDE

Published in 1981 by
Osprey Publishing Ltd
59 Grosvenor Street, London W1X 9DA
© Copyright 1981 Osprey Publishing Ltd
Reprinted 1981 (twice), 1982, 1983 (twice), 1984,
1985, 1986, 1987 (twice), 1988, 1990, 1991

ISBN 0 85045 396 8

Filmset in Great Britain
Printed in Hong Kong

'We are the Pilgrims, Master:
We shall go always a little further:
It may be beyond that last blue mountain barr'd
  with snow,
Across that angry or that glimmering Sea.'
          (From the SAS memorial to their dead;
    22 SAS, Bradbury Lines Camp, Hereford)

**In keeping with security requirements,
photographs showing recent and currently
serving personnel have been masked to
obscure the faces of individual officers and
men.**

Introduction

Since its birth at Kabrit in 1941, the Special Air Service has consistently captured the imagination of the military and public alike by the daring and unconventional nature of its operations. Over a period of 40 years the SAS has found itself in many different theatres of operation, fulfilling many different rôles. Like every other special military force throughout the world, it has been charged with being an 'army within an army', on the grounds of its methods of selection and training and its diversity of skills. The very evident need for such a force would seem to be a complete answer to this charge.

Though its personnel have normally been drawn initially from other units, an SAS regiment has its own distinctive traditions, dress, methods and equipment. The nature of the tasks and the methods peculiar to the SAS have made it difficult to standardise items of equipment. Apart from issues common to the British Army as a whole, SAS personnel have need of, and access to, various specialised 'pieces of kit': often SAS innovations created to meet specific needs. Obvious examples are the 'Lewis bomb' devised by 'L' Detachment in 1941 to meet the needs of their rôle as saboteurs; and the 'stun-grenade' devised by 22 SAS for use in the anti-terrorist rôle nearly four decades later. It has not been possible in all cases to identify the sources of certain items of equipment. In many cases those described or illustrated in this book are of individual choice; their inclusion here should not be taken as meaning that they have been used by, or are available to, every member of the SAS.

Finally, because of the nature of the SAS task, it has not been possible to give 'in-depth' coverage to certain aspects of operations, organization and equipment; and for the same reason it has at times been necessary to refrain from naming individuals.

Since the end of the Second World War members of the SAS have seen service in over 30 different theatres of war and conflict; and since 1950 they have seen continuous action, except for a short period from 1960 to 1963.

Origins

The Special Air Service grew from the Commando movement, the philosophy of carrying the war to the enemy, which itself grew out of the defensive rut into which British military thinking slipped in the aftermath of Dunkirk. The man who lifted it from that rut was a General Staff officer, Lt. Col. Dudley Clarke. In Palestine in 1936 Clarke had seen how small hit-and-run units could tie down an entire army while inflicting damage and demoralising the troops.

In June 1940 Clarke prepared a memo for Sir

Rare photo of an early member of 'L' Detachment, SAS Bde. in Egypt, 1941; the SAS badge is sewn at a slant to the khaki Field Service Cap. (Imperial War Museum)

Western Desert, 1942: David Stirling (right), founder of the SAS, photographed with a raiding patrol of 'L' Detachment, SAS Brigade. This famous study shows officers and men bearded and wearing the Arab-style headcloths they copied from their colleagues in the LRDG. The officer at the wheel of the nearest jeep has a Sykes-Fairbairn commando knife on his left hip, and insignia on his shoulder and left breast, including the 'operational' SAS wings. The jeeps all have modified radiator/condenser systems rigged, and many jerrycans of water and petrol mounted on the bonnet, sides, and in the rear of the body. The patrol leader's jeep mounts twin Vickers K .303 guns; the central jeep, twin and single Vickers guns at front and rear; and the furthest one, a .50cal. Browning—apparently an aircraft weapon— at the front and twin Vickers at the rear. (Imperial War Museum)

John Dill, Chief of the Imperial General Staff, outlining a concept for a small, mobile, offensive fighting force: the concept was based in part on the record of the Boer Kommandos who had tied down a quarter of a million British troops in South Africa. Winston Churchill gave the idea his approval, and by mid-June was asking for 'Storm Troops' or 'Leopards' to be raised from existing units, equipped with priority issues of the latest weapons. Commands throughout the United Kingdom were circularised for volunteers for special service of an undefined but hazardous nature. By the end of June, 180 officers and men

had been assembled, and the trial unit was named 'No. 11 Commando'. Led by Dudley Clarke, they carried out their first cross-Channel raid successfully; and the formation of further units was approved. Against Clarke's wishes the entire operation was begun under the title 'Special Service Battalions', although the similarity to the initials of the Nazi SS was felt too close for comfort.

Churchill's wish to devise ways of hitting back at the enemy, and the impressive seizure of vital objectives by German paratroopers during the European blitzkrieg, led the Prime Minister to order the widening of the commando concept to include the training of a corps of paratroops. By July 1940 Special Service Troops of No. 2 Commando and some members of No. 1 Commando were turned over for parachute training. No. 2 Commando, Special Service Bn. was despatched to Ringway Aerodrome near Manchester for this purpose.

On 21 November 1940, No. 2 Commando was renamed '11 Special Air Service Battalion'. This was a reasonable step, given that it was, as a Commando, a Special Service Bn., and was now assigned to airborne duties. As in the case of Clarke's No. 11 Commando, the title was misleading, perhaps deliberately so, since it implied the existence of ten other SAS battalions. Dudley Clarke is credited with the invention of the name 'Special Air Service'.

During February 1941 'X' Troop from 11 SAS Bn. were parachuted into southern Italy to destroy an aqueduct over the Tragino River, in the first ever British para-commando raid. However, the large-scale German airborne invasion of Crete in May 1941 caused a change of thinking at high level. The concept of para-commandos was downgraded in favour of plans for the airborne delivery of an army—infantry, artillery, engineers and supporting services—all delivered to the battlefield by parachute or glider. It was decided to form two British parachute brigades, one in the UK and one in the Far East. Thus it was that in September 1941, 11 SAS Bn. became 1st Parachute Bn., 2nd and 3rd Bns. being formed subsequently as part of 1st Parachute Brigade. The 2nd Parachute Brigade was formed at Willingdon Airport, New Delhi, consisting of 151st (British), 152nd (Indian) and 153rd (Gurkha) Bns.; and it happened that a consignment of 50 'X'-type parachutes from Britain, destined for India for the use of this formation, somehow found their way into the hands of Lt. Jock Lewis of No. 8 Commando at Alexandria.

'L' Detachment, SAS Brigade

No. 8 Commando was part of 'Layforce', a commando brigade formed in the UK at the end of 1940 to assist British forces in North Africa. The brainchild of Lt.Col. Robert Laycock, it consisted of:

No. 7 Commando …	Formed August 1940
No. 8 Commando …	Formed June 1940 (Brigade of Guards, Royal Marines and Somerset Light Infantry personnel)
Special Boat Section …	Formed Arran, Scotland, in June 1940, with two officers and 15 men, and sent to Middle East with 8 Cdo.
No. 11 Commando …	Scottish commando, formed late 1940
Nos. 50 & 52 Cdos. …	Two small forces of mixed Army and RM, raised in Middle East, early 1941.

Jeep patrol mounted by members of the Greek 'Sacred Squadron' in the Libyan Desert, 1942. The 'Sacred Squadron' was absorbed by the SAS in March of that year. (Imperial War Museum)

Member of the Special Boat Service on operations in the Aegean, 1943–44. He wears the beige beret, and is seen here sharpening his commando knife. Note US M1 carbine at his feet. See Plate B2. (Imperial War Museum)

GHQ Middle East was hesitant to use Layforce in its raiding rôle because of shortage of ships. A young Scots Guards subaltern serving with No. 8 Cdo., David Stirling, felt that if delivery of commandos by sea was not possible, then perhaps delivery by parachute was. When his friend Jock Lewis obtained Laycock's permission to experiment with parachuting, Stirling applied to join the venture. None of the commandos were parachute-trained, and in June 1941 no parachute school existed in the Middle East. Lewis, Stirling and six other commandos conducted their training at Mersa Matruh airfield, using an ancient Valencia bomber. In due course Stirling, with a damaged spine and temporarily paralysed legs, found himself in the Scottish Military Hospital in Alexandria.

He put his enforced idleness to good use, expanding on paper his ideas on airborne commando operations. He felt that the current concept of a force of some 200 men landing without warning from the sea was unsound, since the size of the force often meant that the element of surprise was lost, and a third of the force was immediately tied down in securing the landing area.

He proposed that instead of mounting attacks from the sea on the long coastal plain where most of the fighting was taking place, strikes should be mounted on enemy airfields and installations from the southern, desert flank. Instead of a large force, Stirling visualised a maximum force of 60 men divided into four-man units, parachuted into the desert close to an objective. They would hide until nightfall, and then carry out their sabotage raid, falling back into the desert to rendezvous with a patrol which would transport them back to Allied lines.

After his discharge from hospital in July, Stirling took his plan to HQ Middle East Command, and by guile and determination managed to reach the office of the Deputy Commander, Gen. Ritchie. His plan appealed to both Ritchie and the C-in-C, Gen. Auchinleck. New to his command, Auchinleck was under pressure from Churchill to mount an offensive, and operations of the kind outlined by Stirling would both ease this pressure and materially assist his general offensive when he was ready to launch it.

Layforce was earmarked for disbandment; the shortage of ships had not been overcome. Of its component units, 11 Cdo. had lost 25 per cent of its strength in Syria in June 1941, and rearguard actions on Crete had also cost 7, 50 and 52 Cdos. and elements of 8 Cdo. dearly; 8 Cdo. had also been used at Tobruk. Some personnel were being shipped home, while others were retained as 'Middle East Commando' after Layforce was finally disbanded at the end of 1941. (The unsuccessful raid to kill or capture Rommel mounted by 59 men of 11 Cdo. under Lt.Col. Geoffrey Keyes on 17/18 November was the last example of Dudley Clarke's original commando concept; henceforth commandos would be used as special assault troops in the van of general offensives.)

Auchinleck authorised Stirling to recruit 66 commandos from Layforce, from which formation they would take their title, 'L' Detachment. Since they would be para-commandos, their 'higher formation' would be known as the Special Air Service Brigade, although no such formation actually existed. Brigadier Dudley Clarke was engaged in deceiving the Axis into the belief that the British had paratroop capability in the Middle East, by planting dummy gliders for enemy air reconnaissance to photograph, and by dropping dummy paratroops near Axis POW camps and in sight of pro-Axis Arabs. At this time—July 1941— the paratroops in the UK were still called '11 Special Air Service Bn.', so the use of the SAS title by Stirling was logical. The general promoted Stirling to captain, and parted from him with the words: 'Whatever comes from your project, your presence will greatly relieve Clarke's burden.' With this limited objective, the SAS was born.

From 'L' Detachment to 1st SAS

Capt. Stirling set out to recruit his 66 men; and within a week the six officers, five NCOs and 55 men—most of them from Layforce—assembled at Kabrit, at the edge of the Great Bitter Lake in the Suez Canal Zone. The original officers were Lewis, Thomas, Bonnington, Fraser, McGonigal and 'Paddy' Mayne. When recruited Mayne was under close arrest for striking his commanding officer. The same uninhibited attitude was evident in 'L' Detachment's first raid. Kabrit proved to consist of three tents, a few chairs, a table and a painted sign. A large camp of New Zealanders two miles away quickly but involuntarily provided a more realistic scale of issue, packed into a 3-ton truck under cover of darkness.

Training started immediately, aimed at promoting a high level of skill at navigation and night movement, and the handling of Allied and Axis weapons. There was also improvised 'jump' training. Since no timber was available from the QM department for making a para-training platform, Stirling and his men trained by performing backward rolls off the back of the 3-tonner at 30mph. Several appeals to Parachute Training School One at Ringway for advice on various aspects of parachute training went unanswered, so the SAS was unable to draw on Ringway's experience. This may have contributed to the deaths of two troopers during subsequent training: when the SAS started making jumps from an RAF Bristol Bombay, two men died when the static lines of their 'chutes failed—an accident of which Ringway already had experience.

'L' Detachment was, predictably, the target of some sniping from elements of GHQ who considered such 'side shows' a waste of time. When an RAF officer voiced this opinion, Stirling bet him that the SAS could penetrate Heliopolis, the main RAF airbase outside Cairo. In a useful dummy-run for their raids against Luftwaffe and Reggia Aeronautica bases, 40 SAS men set off across the desert by different routes. They reached the base 90 miles away, penetrated the perimeter, stuck labels on the aircraft, and slipped out without detection.

In the months leading up to Auchinleck's November offensive Stirling and Lewis spent hours at a time studying maps, intelligence reports and logistic problems. The plan was for a parachute attack on five German forward airfields holding the bulk of the Luftwaffe's fighters. For the raid Jock Lewis invented a special sabotage weapon, a combined blast and incendiary charge, calculated to do the maximum damage to aircraft; made of thermite and plastic explosive, it was called the Lewis bomb.

Tragically, the first operational jump against the airfields on 16 November 1941 was a disaster. A moonless night and high desert winds completely disrupted the jump. The plan was for 62 officers and men in five parties to be dropped from Bristol Bombays near the five airfields; after destroying the aircraft on the fields they were to rendezvous with the Long Range Desert Group for ferrying

SBS soldier in 'woolly pully' and beige beret with SAS badge, photographed outside HQ Raiding Forces Middle East; the SBS operated under this headquarters from November 1943. (Imperial War Museum)

Rhodesian members of the British SAS regiments pose with a jeep modified for use by SAS in NW Europe. The front seats and twin Vickers K gun mount are armoured and have armour-glass windshields. A Bren is mounted on the wing beside the driver. The gunner wears a maroon beret; a Denison smock; despatch rider's boots with turned-down socks and a commando knife stuck in the top; and a holstered pistol slung low on the hip. Tank driver's gauntlets are worn by two of this group. (SAS Regt. Assoc.)

back to Allied lines. In the event, only 22 officers and men returned from the raid, including Stirling. He abandoned the idea of parachuting into the desert, and devised instead the idea of 'infiltration' and 'exfiltration' by the LRDG.

The Long Range Desert Group was born in June 1940, primarily as an intelligence-gathering unit, and was the brainchild of Ralph Bagnold. Its members became experts at living in, and navigating across, the desert at great ranges and under all conditions. The primary means of transport was the specially modified 30cwt Chevrolet truck, and heavy machine gun armament was carried, since the LRDG not infrequently found itself fighting it out with the enemy on the ground and in the air.

In November 1941 Gen. Ritchie, now C-in-C 8th Army, approved the move of 'L' Detachment SAS to Jalo Oasis, where it operated with a squadron of the LRDG. It was obviously necessary to wipe out the failure of the first raid with a quick success, if the hostile elements at GHQ were not to succeed in burying the whole concept. In December Stirling's men were ferried to and from raids on three enemy airfields at Sirte, Agheila and Agedabia; the raids were a total success, and 'L' Detachment were credited with destroying some 61 aircraft and 30 vehicles with Lewis bombs. Just before Christmas 1941 another attack was

mounted: Stirling and Mayne would attack airfields at Sirte and Tamit, while Lewis attacked one at Nofilia. Both Mayne's and Lewis's parties were successful in blowing up aircraft, though Lewis was killed during the return trip. Stirling's group reached Sirte late, and were unable to plant their bombs. Their improvised response to this situation was to prove so successful that it was used in the future: a motorised charge down the airstrip, blazing away at the aircraft with machine guns and grenades from the back of the LRDG trucks. By the time they returned to Kabrit 'L' Detachment had destroyed 90 aircraft.

Promoted major in January 1942, Stirling was empowered to enlarge, re-organize and re-equip 'L' Detachment. Among other recruits he arranged to acquire the services of a company of Free French paratroopers, 50 men under Capt. Bergé, who had begun life as the 1e Compagnie d'Infanterie de l'Air in Britain, and who were now designated 1e Compagnie de Chasseurs Parachutistes (1e CCP).

Stirling now consolidated the identity of his SAS by having unit insignia designed and made up—the hostility of GHQ to such a step being side-stepped by obtaining the blessing of the C-in-C himself. The colours chosen for insignia were dark blue and light 'Pompadour' blue, referring to the Oxford and Cambridge rowing background of two of the original officers, Lewis and Langton. The cap badge was originally designed as a flaming 'sword of Damocles' over a motto summing up Stirling's SAS concept: 'Who Dares Wins'. Made up by a Cairo tailor, the flaming sword actually appeared as a winged dagger, and the wings were retained and formalised as a fitting element in the unit's heraldry. A pair of parachute qualification wings in white and two tones of blue were also manufactured, and issued after seven jumps; they were worn on the right upper arm. For conspicuous operational service certain SAS men were allowed to transfer them to the left breast.[1] Jock Lewis is credited with the design of these insignia before his death.

The new cap badge on its dark blue shield-

[1] This practice continued until stopped after the war by the Army Council, who decreed that only the Army Air Corps and Glider Pilot Regt. should wear breast wings. SAS wings on the breast were thus a sign of very early and distinguished service in the unit.

shaped patch was sewn on all kinds of headgear—Field Service caps, Service Dress caps, and even French *képis*—replacing the previously worn insignia of the men's original parent units. The SAS also sought a new uniform and headgear. An early scheme to adopt a smart light blue uniform styled on that of the New Zealand Air Force was abandoned. There was some initial use of a white beret, modelled on the headgear of 1ᵉ CCP, but this was found to provoke fights in Cairo, particularly with ANZACS! In its place a beige-coloured beret was finally adopted. Until January 1944, when the SAS Brigade was formed under 1st Airborne Division, the SAS had no other insignia apart from those described.

Stirling's plans to widen the rôle of the SAS brought the Special Boat Section of No. 8 Commando into the SAS orbit, when a raid was planned on shipping in Bouerat harbour.

Sometimes called the Folboat Section (after their collapsible canoes), this unit was raised in July 1940 under Lt. Roger Courtney; the plan was to have a section of some 30 men with each Commando, for intelligence gathering prior to commando assaults. In February 1941 the SBS was divided and Courtney took 16 men to No. 8 Cdo. and the Middle East. The remainder were sent to Dover, and in November became 'SBS 101 Troop' attached to No. 6 Commando.

The SBS wore a black shoulder title with red lettering 'Commando SBS'; below this was a blue and white shield patch with a motif of Excalibur being held up from the water by the Lady of the Lake, and red lettering 'SBS'. The Dover troop wore, from November 1941, a red-on-black 'No. 6 Commando' title above a blue rectangular patch bearing a white swordfish swimming through a red '101'; the swordfish badge was also produced in metal.

The Commando Special Boat Section has often been confused with the SAS Special Boat Squadron, and later SAS Special Boat Service, because of the common cypher. (These units should not be confused, equally, with the 'RM Special Boat Sections'—see later passage under main heading 'RM Special Boat Squadron'.)

The joint SAS/SBS raid on Bouerat took place in January 1942; again they were inserted by the LRDG, but unfortunately the canoe was damaged in transit. Nevertheless, severe damage was done to the harbour, stores and petrol tankers by the SAS party. Late in March Stirling tried a similar attack on Benghazi harbour, again with limited success due to boat damage, although Mayne managed to destroy 15 aircraft at Berka.

In March Stirling managed to have the Greek 'Sacred Squadron' attached to 'L' Detachment. The *Helios Lokos* was formed from ex-officers of the Greek Army who had escaped the German occupation of their country; led by Col. Gigantes, they were part of the New Zealand Corps. They were immediately put on the SAS training course which the 1ᵉ CCP, now the 'French Squadron SAS', had just completed.

In June 1942 yet another small unit came under Stirling's ambit: the Special Interrogation Group or SIG. This extremely misleading title concealed a unit of anti-Nazi Germans, mostly Palestinian Jews of German origin, formed by a Captain Herbert Buck, an Indian Army officer. The SIG, whose training was up to SAS standards on selection, were dressed and equipped entirely with captured German Army items. They spoke German, carried German documentation, and lived their everyday life exactly like Afrika Korps personnel. Stirling recruited the SIG's services for a very special raid.

To prevent the Luftwaffe from sinking a vitally-needed convoy sailing for Malta, eight groups of five men were briefed to attack aircraft on fields at Derna, Barce, Benghazi, and Heraklion on Crete. Unfortunately the raid did not go as planned, and

Brigadier Mike Calvert (right) with Rhodesian SAS men in NW Europe. A fairly piratical mixture of clothing is evident; despatch rider's breeches and boots seem popular, and one soldier (third from right) has acquired a Luftwaffe flying jacket. Note SAS badge painted on rear right body of jeep, far left. (SAS Regt. Assoc.)

4 May 1945: men of 2 SAS attend an open-air mass to celebrate the end of the war in Europe, in the Italian town of Cuneo. Apart from two men (rear left) retaining beige berets, the maroon Airborne headgear is worn. A mixture of Denison smocks and hooded windproofs is evident here, and short puttees are clearly preferred to webbing anklets. Pistol holsters are slung low in most cases, and some are strapped down to the thigh. (Imperial War Museum)

losses were high. The Crete patrol was led by Cdt. Bergé, with two other Frenchmen, the Earl Jellicoe, and a Greek Sacred Squadron officer as guide. Enormous damage was done to the airfield, but only Jellicoe escaped.

The other parties did varying amounts of damage. The SIG accompanied three French patrols, acting as guards escorting French 'prisoners'. Unfortunately a traitor in the SIG betrayed part of this group, which was targeted on four airfields around Derna, and most of that unit were wiped out. This was a blow from which the SIG did not recover.

An important addition to the SAS armoury was the heavily-armed jeep. From the RAF, Stirling managed to obtain a number of Vickers 'K' .303 machine guns, a drum-fed weapon which could be mounted in pairs. At about this time a raid on Bagush airfield had nearly failed when half the planted bombs failed to explode; the SAS remedied the situation by driving around the field shooting up the 40 aircraft. Now Stirling managed to obtain numbers of jeeps, and these were fitted with twin Vickers front and rear, and with a modified radiator system for desert use. Later the armament was supplemented by the addition of Browning .50cal. heavy machine guns. The jeeps gave the SAS their own mobility, and enabled them to raid at will.

In August 1942 the Special Boat Section of Middle East Commando came under SAS control, and Earl Jellicoe and Fitzroy Maclean organized within the SAS what would emerge as the SAS Special Boat Squadron. SBS members were full members of the SAS, qualified to wear the wings and the sand beret. Maclean was given command of 'M' Detachment, SBS, intended for operations behind enemy lines if Germany invaded Persia and Iraq.[1] When the threat receded Maclean was transferred to other duties—parachuted into Yugoslavia, he was a senior British representative with Tito's partisans. His detachment of SAS/SBS was taken over by Ian Lapraik; other units were

[1] The threat of this was considerably reduced when Fitzroy Maclean calmly kidnapped the pro-Axis chief of the Persian general staff from his office in Teheran.

'L' (Langton) and 'S' (Sutherland) Detachments. In September 1942 the SAS/SBS began operations with an attack on the island of Rhodes, destroying aircraft and stores.

In October 1942 the clearly outmoded title of 'L' Detachment was dropped in favour of 1st Special Air Service (1 SAS), a regiment in its own right; at that time its strength was 390 all ranks. In November the disbandment of Middle East Commando allowed Stirling to recruit another ten officers and 100 men.

From Regiment to Brigade

Stirling's command now comprised the following elements:

1 SAS	...	500 all ranks
French SAS Sqn. (1ᵉ CCP)	...	94 all ranks
Greek Sacred Squadron	...	114 all ranks
Special Boat Section (later, Squadron)	...	55 all ranks

Plans were now laid for the formation of a second SAS regiment under command of David Stirling's brother, William; 2 SAS would be formed out of 62 Cdo. in North-West Africa. 2 SAS did not officially exist until May 1943, but it was already training with 1st Army, which had landed in Africa in Operation 'Torch' in November 1942.

In January 1943 Lt.Col. David Stirling was captured by a German counter-SAS unit in the Sfax-Gabes area. After four escape attempts he eventually ended the war at Colditz Castle. Command of 1 SAS passed to Major Paddy Mayne, as the war in North Africa drew to a close. During the course of its operations the SAS had destroyed nearly 400 enemy aircraft—more than even the RAF had achieved.

April 1943 brought the break-up of what had been Stirling's North Africa command, and the next year saw a complex pattern of re-organization. The French Squadron returned to Britain; in July, with another company of French paratroopers formed in Africa, it became 1ᵉ BIA (Bataillon d'Infanterie de l'Air), and shortly thereafter was redesignated 4ᵉ BIA. It was joined by a 3ᵉ BIA formed in Africa. Later still, the 3ᵉ and 4ᵉ BIA were re-named 2ᵉ and 3ᵉ Régiments de Chasseurs Parachutistes—2ᵉ and 3ᵉ RCP.

1 SAS was split in two. The 250 men of 'B' Squadron under Earl Jellicoe became the Special Boat Squadron, absorbing the Special Boat Section and also the Small Scale Raiding Force. (This SSRF, formed in 1941, had operated under joint control of the Chief of Combined Operations and the Special Operations Executive, seeing action off the coasts of France and Africa; it had become part of No. 62 Cdo. in January 1943.)

The SBS were based at Athlit near Haifa. With the Greek Sacred Squadron they raided enemy-occupied Mediterranean and Aegean islands. In November it was one of the units placed under command of Brig. D. J. T. Turnbull's Raiding Forces Middle East as part of XIII Corps. Later retitled Special Boat Service, the SBS was to come under Land Forces Adriatic for continuing operations with the Greek Sacred Squadron in the Mediterranean, Aegean and Adriatic Seas.

The former 'A' Squadron, 1 SAS became the 'Special Raiding Squadron', still led by Paddy Mayne. In July 1943 the SRS played a spearhead rôle in Operation 'Husky', the invasion of Sicily; and during the next few months it was used on commando lines against enemy positions along the

Lt.Col. Paddy (Blair) Mayne, the Irish commanding officer of 1 SAS, at a parade in 1945; he still retains the beige beret. He wears officer's No. 2 Dress with a Sam Browne belt, minus cross strap; plain leather buttons; the blue left shoulder lanyard adopted by this regiment; and 'operational' SAS breast wings. (SAS Regt. Assoc.)

1 October 1945: Brigadier Mike Calvert, Commandant SAS Bde., at the ceremony marking the passing of 3 and 4 SAS (2e and 3e RCP) from the British to the French Army. A mixture of insignia can be seen here; see also Plate B3. Some soldiers wear Free French para wings on the right breast, others SAS 'operational' wings on the left. The maroon berets are worn in both the British manner (pulled right) and the French (pulled left). The Pegasus arm patch of British 1st Airborne Div. can be seen in the nearest rank. (Imperial War Museum)

Mediterranean coasts, and on mainland Italy. SRS suffered heavy losses in October 1943 at Termoli, when, alongside 3 Cdo. and 40 RM Cdo., they ran into the German 1st Parachute Division.

Meanwhile 2 SAS was officially inaugurated in May 1943, based at Philippeville in Algeria. They raided Sardinia, Sicily, and the Italian mainland, led by Lt.Col. William Stirling. Stirling complained to his superiors that the SAS was not being used for the job for which it had trained, suggesting that small sabotage groups parachuted behind enemy lines would be more effective. 2 SAS progressed up Italy, eventually meeting up with SRS (ex-1 SAS) at Termoli.

At the end of 1943 Special Raiding Squadron reverted to the title 1 SAS; with 2 SAS it was pulled out of its commando rôle and placed under command of 1st Airborne Division. In January 1944 the idea of an SAS Brigade was approved; and in March, after further action in the Italian theatre, 1 and 2 SAS were sent back to Britain. The Brigade would consist of:

1 SAS (British and Commonwealth)
2 SAS (British and Commonwealth)
3 SAS (French)—French designation 2e RCP
4 SAS (French)—French designation 3e RCP
Independent Belgian Squadron (subsequently 5 SAS)
'F' Sqn., GHQ Regt. (HQ, signals and communications)

The Brigade was formed in Ayrshire in January 1944, only the French and Belgian elements being present before the arrival of 1 and 2 SAS from the Mediterranean: command was held by Brig. Roderick McLeod.

The Belgian squadron had led the chequered career common to many exile units. They had started life as 'B' Coy., 2nd Belgian Fusilier Bn. in May 1942. Sent for para-training in October, they were subsequently attached to 3rd Bn., Parachute Regiment. January 1943 saw them redesignated Belgian Independent Parachute Company, and August 1943, 4 Coy., 8th Bn., Parachute Regiment.

'F' Sqn. came from a unit known variously as the GHQ Liaison Regiment, or 'Phantom'. Founded by Lt.Col. G. F. Hopkinson, 'Phantom' was an intelligence, reconnaissance and signals unit; its task was to gather intelligence in forward areas and behind enemy lines, and to radio the information back to GHQ. Its members included several names later to become famous, among them the future HM Government ministers Maurice Macmillan and Hugh Fraser, and the film actor David Niven. 'F' Sqn. of the regiment was assigned to the SAS Brigade, and was commanded by Major J. J. Astor. Two patrols each were assigned to 1 and 2 SAS. The French and Belgian units had their own signallers, but these were retrained along 'Phantom' lines and then returned to their units to work directly with 'F' Sqn. All 'F' Sqn. personnel wore a white 'P' ('Phantom') shoulder flash.

By March 1944 all components of the SAS Brigade, 2,000 strong, were assembled in Ayrshire. The SAS were ordered to discard their beige berets in favour of airborne maroon. They were also issued with battledress shoulder titles for 1, 2, 3 and 4 SAS in the airborne colours of pale blue on maroon. Col. Mayne, CO of 1 SAS, was only one of many SAS men who risked censure by stubbornly retaining the beige beret. (1 SAS also seems to have adopted a dark blue lanyard on the left shoulder at this time. Most SAS men wore lanyards in the colours of their parent regiments, if any.)

The French and Belgians, who had trained with Airborne Forces prior to the creation of the Brigade, also wore the light-blue-on-maroon 'Pegasus' arm patch. The two French regiments did not, for the most part, bother to wear their SAS shoulder titles, but continued to wear white-on-black 'France' titles. They wore a Free French style of parachutist's wings ('brevet') on the right breast—white parachute and wings supporting a yellow shield with a blue Cross of Lorraine. The Belgians wore the British SAS wings.

In the early days of the Brigade Lt.Col. William Stirling, CO of 2 SAS, resigned. He felt that the SAS was once more being misused, and his brother's concept ignored. He had seen his men used as commando assault troops in Sicily and Italy, and now they were being turned into something little different from conventional paratroops. The whole concept of small sabotage groups was being lost. Stirling was succeeded by Lt.Col. Brian Franks as CO of 2 SAS. On operations, HQ SAS Bde. had to liaise with a series of different headquarters: 46 or 38 Group RAF, SOE HQ (Special Forces), and 1st Airborne Division.

The new style of operations planned for the SAS on mainland Europe was attended by a new danger. During the height of the commando raids Hitler had issued orders that captured commandos were to be shot. As a result of the success

1945: a group of soldiers from 1 SAS photographed after an investiture. Only three wear the 'official' maroon beret. Best battledress and blancoed webbing are worn here; the pale-blue-on-maroon '1st SAS' shoulder title, and the regiment's blue lanyard, are worn by all these men, as are the 'operational' breast wings. (SAS Regt. Assoc.)

Rare photograph of Lt.Col. Ian Lapraik with men of the early 21st SAS Regt. (Artists) (v) emplaning for a parachute jump in the early 1950s. Most wear SAS hooded camouflage smocks and matching trousers. Col. Lapraik (right) can be seen to wear the 'Mars and Minerva' cap badge on the maroon beret, and the '21st Special Air Service'/(Artists)' shoulder title; see also Plate D1. (21 SAS)

of SAS operations the Führer issued a special order that captured SAS troops were to be handed over to the Gestapo, interrogated, and then 'ruthlessly exterminated'.

The SAS was not again committed to action until the invasion of Normandy in June 1944. Neither SHAEF nor 21st Army Group—primarily responsible for the 'Overlord' operations—were prepared to take direct command of the SAS, despite the Brigade's vast experience. In fact 21st Army Group blocked the use of the SAS until after 'Overlord' had begun. A very limited rôle for SAS was outlined: the Brigade's job would be to prevent German reserves reaching the front line. Initially only half the brigade would be committed, the remainder being held in reserve. After D-Day the SAS carried out a number of operations behind enemy lines which disrupted German supplies and communications and tied down large numbers of enemy troops.

The early operations in this phase of the war involved both clandestine penetration of the front lines, and air-drops deep in enemy-occupied

country. Bases were set up in remote wooded countryside, and all re-supply was by air. There was close liaison with local resistance groups. A great deal of damage was done to enemy communications, sometimes for little cost, and on other occasions at the price of heavy SAS casualties. There was bound to be a strong element of chance, since the parties worked in a fluid situation with very variable intelligence information, and their security was easily compromised. Examples of successful operations included Operation 'Houndsworth', carried out between D-Day and 6 September 1944 by 144 officers and men of 1 SAS. Railway lines between Lyons and Chalon-sur-Saone, Dijon and Paris, and Le Creusot and Nevers were cut 22 times, and some 350 casualties were inflicted on the Germans. In the same period Operation 'Bullbasket', launched by 56 men of 1 SAS and 3 Phantom Patrol south of Chateauroux, achieved a good measure of success; but the group were betrayed to the enemy, and 36 men died before the survivors could be extracted by air early in August. In the second and third weeks of June 150 men of the French SAS battalions co-operated with up to 3,000 Maquis fighters in Operation 'Dingson'; the SAS base was heavily attacked by the enemy, and the group was forced to disperse on 18 June.

While audacious use of the armed and armoured jeeps with which the SAS groups were normally equipped achieved excellent results through the element of surprise, it must be recorded that some groups got carried away by their own bravado, bringing down on themselves and on the local population severe enemy reaction.

In late 1944 members of 2 SAS were parachuted into Italy in Operation 'Tombola', to work with Italian partisans; they remained there until Italy was liberated. The remainder of the SAS were to work with local resistance groups in a series of operations which took them into France, Belgium, Holland and finally Germany.

In March 1945 Brig. McLeod was posted to India, his post as Commandant of SAS Brigade passing to Brig. 'Mad Mike' Calvert. A former 'Chindit' brigadier under Maj.Gen. Orde Wingate behind Japanese lines in Burma, Calvert was an expert on guerilla warfare and long-range penetration.

In April 1945, their ranks swelled with recruits from liberated Belgium, the Belgian Squadron became 5 SAS. Their three squadrons worked with 2nd Canadian Corps in a reconnaissance rôle in northern Holland and Germany.

The war in Europe ended on 8 May 1945. By this date some 330 casualties had been suffered by the Brigade, which had killed or seriously wounded 7,733 of the enemy, and captured nearly 23,000. In May, 1 and 2 SAS were sent to Norway to supervise the surrender of 300,000 German troops; at the same time 5 SAS were involved in counter-intelligence work in Denmark and Germany.

The war against Japan was still raging, however, and under Brig. Calvert the SAS looked to South-East Asia for its new deployment. David Stirling had now been freed from Colditz, and was back with the SAS planning for operations against the Japanese along the Manchurian Railway. The former Commandant of SAS Bde., Brig. McLeod, was now Director of Military Operations at GHQ New Delhi, and would certainly appreciate the use of the SAS in the East. The surrender of the Japanese in August pre-empted this plan, however.

For clarity, a short note is relevant here on two 'SAS-style' units which did see action in the Far East. The French had raised a unit entitled 'Special Air Service Bataillon B' in India and Ceylon. Under its initial title of Light Intervention Corps (CLI), part of this unit had been dropped into Japanese-held Laos to assist guerillas against the enemy. The CLI was based in Ceylon in May 1945, and, renamed SAS Bn. 'B', it became part of an *ad hoc* formation entitled 5th Colonial Infantry Regiment. This also included naval personnel, including a parachute-commando group named after its commander, 'Ponchardier'. These French troops, used for the re-occupation of French Indo-China, were never linked in any way to the British SAS.

Commando Special Boat Sections also operated in the Far East from June 1944 until VJ-Day as part of Small Operations Group, which had been formed by Lt.Col. Hasler of the Royal Marines, and was commanded in the Far East by Col. Tollemache.

The 'tree-jumping' kit used in Malaya. Note rope attached to parachute harness; maroon beret with SAS badge tucked into harness; SAS para-wings just visible on right shoulder of jungle-green bush shirt; and sleeveless jump-jerkin worn over personal equipment and under harness. (Imperial War Museum)

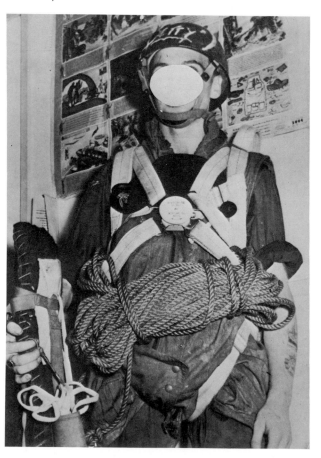

The Post-War SAS

With the war over, the British Army's ostensible need for, and tolerance of, such 'private armies' as the SAS was apparently over; and the peacetime army wasted little time in dismantling the SAS Brigade. On 8 October 1945 1 SAS, 2 SAS and HQ SAS were disbanded.

On 21 September 1945 the Belgian 5 SAS was handed over by Brig. Calvert to the Belgian Army. After some uncertainty it was based at Westmalle as the Belgian Army's 1st Parachute Bn. (SAS). Personnel from this unit served between 1950 and 1954 in the Corps Voluntaire Corée in the Korean War. In 1952 a battalion was formed from what had been the Belgian contingent in the British No. 10 Cdo.; together 1st Para Bn. (SAS) and 2nd Cdo. Bn. formed the Belgian Para-Commando Regiment, with HQ at Namur. In 1955 the 3rd Bn. was formed from the former CVC, and 4th, 5th and 6th Bns. were formed at various times during the troubles in the Belgian Congo. The 1st Para Bn. (SAS) saw action in the Congo at various times before and after independence. The Para-Commando Regiment now has three battalions: 1st Bn. personnel wear a metal winged sword badge on a maroon beret, and both 1st and 3rd wear a similar metal badge at the shoulder. Uniforms and insignia otherwise conform to normal Belgian issue. The SAS connection has been no more than traditional since the immediate post-war period, and the unit is a conventional paratroop battalion.

The same is true of the French SAS. On 1 October 1945, 3 and 4 SAS were handed over to the French Army, reverting to their titles of 2^e and 3^e RCP. Demobilisation and amalgamation left a single unit, entitled 2e RCP. In July 1945 the French Committee of National Defence had decided to form two SAS-type parachute battalions for service in Indo-China; and in November it was decided to form a Group of three battalions, under command of Lt.Col. de Bollardière, former CO of the 2e RCP. In fact only two battalions were ever formed. The 1st SAS Bn. (originally, $1/1^{er}$ RCP), formed from members of the wartime 1er RCP and the post-war 2e RCP, was commanded by Maj. Mollat, and landed in Indo-China in February 1946. The 2nd SAS Bn. (originally, $2/2^e$ RCP) was led by Maj. de Maurepas, formerly of the 2^e RCP, and landed in June 1946.

In July the two units were brought together into the Demi-Brigade SAS, and subsequently saw heavy combat against the Viet-Minh all over French Indo-China. They fought as conventional air-mobile intervention troops. The DBSAS was subsequently retitled Demi-Brigade Coloniale de Commandos Parachutistes (DBCCP), and the SAS identity was retained only in a traditional sense. Broken up to form separate Colonial Parachute Battalions in 1952, the Demi-Brigade represents a stage in the complex evolution of French airborne forces which later allowed four units to incorporate the SAS cypher or motto in their regimental badges: the 1er, 2^e, 6^e and 7^e RPIMa. (It should be emphasised that units of an entirely different type and rôle were operational in Algeria during that country's war of independence from the French—the Sections Administratives Speciales—whose common 'SAS' cypher is sometimes confused with that of the Special Air Service.)

It is perhaps worth mentioning that it was a former member of the French wartime SAS, Capt. Maidec, who organized the North African guerilla warfare training school, laying down doctrines followed in the early 1960s during the transformation of the Foreign Legion's 2nd Parachute Regiment (2e REP) into an élite intervention unit, which today has special skills to some extent paralleling those of 22 SAS. In recent years 1er RPIMa has also trained in some SAS-type rôles.

The RSM of 22 SAS with NCOs; Malaya, 1956. He wears 'pea greens', and his NCOs the white No. 3 Dress—see Plate E2. (22 SAS)

In Greece the defeat of Germany led to an attempt by the Communist organization ELAS to seize power by force. A bitter civil war broke out between Greeks who had fought together against the foreign occupiers during the war, and British troops were committed in support of the legitimate government. The Greek Sacred Squadron and some elements of the Special Boat Service, with whom they had been operating against the Germans and Italians in the eastern Mediteranean, were among the units to see action. When they were no longer needed the SBS were returned to England and disbanded. The Sacred Squadron were also disbanded when the threat of ELAS was averted; but today's Greek Army includes a Ranger Raider Force which directly continues the traditions of the Squadron. A shoulder patch bears an upward-pointing winged sword—recalling the badge of the Sacred Squadron and their SAS associations—and the Greek language motto 'Who Dares Wins'.

1st Special Air Service Regiment

In 1946 a War Office Tactical Investigation Committee looking into the possible use of commando and SAS-type units in a future European conflict decided (against some formidable opposition from senior elements of the Regular Army) that such troops had a rôle. The Royal Marines would be responsible for short-term shallow penetration with support from commando-trained Army specialists; and for longer-term deep penetration an SAS regiment was to be raised as part of the Territorial Army, under a Corps Warrant. Apart from placing the regiment firmly in the British Army 'order of battle', the warrant was important in that it allowed for subsequent raising of further SAS regiments up to a total of approximately 10,000 men.

There was much intricate manoeuvring over a choice of title for the unit, and eventually it emerged as 21st SAS Regiment (v). The actual regiment chosen to receive the SAS mantle was a distinguished old volunteer unit, the Artists' Rifles. Raised in 1860 by Edward Sterling from 'practitioners of the Arts', the regiment formed part of the Rifle Brigade, and wore certain green and black uniform accoutrements in Rifles style. They chose as their cap badge the heads of Mars, God of War, and Minerva, Goddess of Wisdom. A succession of redesignations followed. The 28th Bn. London Regiment (Artists' Rifles) saw distinguished service in the First World War, providing ordinary ranks for commissioning as officers in other units. In 1937 it was transferred from 2nd Brigade (London) to a new formation, the 'Officer Producing Unit', with the title

Members of 22 SAS mount a Guard of Honour for inspection by an RAF officer; Malaya, 1956. They wear No. 6 Dress with maroon berets and Malaya Command patches. The officer (left foreground) wears SAS wings on his shoulder, and 'SAS' cyphers on his shoulderstraps. (22 SAS)

shortened to simply 'The Artists' Rifles'.

Lt.Col. Brian Franks, formerly CO of 2 SAS, became the first commanding officer of 21st Special Air Service Regiment (Artists) (Volunteers) when it came into existence on 1 January 1947. 21 SAS took over the old Artists' Rifles HQ at Duke's Road, Euston; many of the first recruits were wartime SAS veterans, who brought with them their experience and traditions.

During the Korean War a United Nations Partisan Infantry Korea (UNPIK) force was formed in a special forces rôle, making a number of parachute drops into North Korea. It consisted mainly of US Rangers, with some Korean personnel and some British volunteers. The 'British end' has in the past been mistaken for an SAS operation, but this is not the case. Members of the 21st SAS were destined for Korea at one time, however. General Macarthur requested Britain to provide an SAS force, and a special unit of squadron strength was formed in 1950 from the 'Z' reserve of 21 SAS, under Major Anthony Greville-Bell. It never reached Korea, due to the parallel development of a similar task for British forces in Malaya, and was later redesignated 'M' (for Malaya) Squadron and re-assigned for duties with the Malayan Scouts in Johore under 'Mad Mike' Calvert.

The Malayan Scouts (Special Air Service)

In April 1948 a series of murders marked the beginning of a Communist uprising in Malaya.

Following decisions taken at the 1948 Calcutta International Congress, ten battalions of guerillas moved back into the Malayan jungle with weapons left over from wartime operations against the Japanese, and launched their war on European colonialism. British Regular troops, and six Gurkha battalions, were soon employed in a jungle war.

In July 1948 an anti-terrorist unit called Ferret Force was formed for operations in Malaya. It consisted of Iban Dyak trackers from Borneo, and former members of Force 136: this had been a wartime SOE group operating in the Far East. One of these was Major Dare Newell, later a 22 SAS adjutant and present SAS Association Secretary. Ferret Force had a short but very successful career, and by the time it was disbanded, because its military personnel were needed elsewhere, it had shown up the drastic need for special forces in the region. By 1950 the Communist offensive was going from strength to strength; and the C-in-C Far East, Gen. Sir John Harding, called Mike Calvert from his staff posting in Hong Kong. Perhaps the greatest expert on guerilla warfare then serving in the British Army, Calvert had reverted from his wartime rank of brigadier to his substantive rank of major after the disbandment of the SAS Brigade in 1945. At Harding's request he toured the affected area of Malaya for six months, and came up with a two-part plan.

The first part involved the removal of the populations of outlying villages into protected stockades in safer locations, together with strict monitoring of personal movement and food supplies. The guerillas ('CTs', 'Communist terrorists') would thus be denied food and shelter, and would be hampered in any attempts to coerce the civil population. The second part was the creation of a special forces unit which would live in the jungle, pursuing the CTs and winning the 'hearts and minds' of the aboriginal tribes. In June 1951 Harding's Director of Operations, Gen. Sir Harold Briggs, put the first part of the plan into operation with the uprooting of 410 villages. Calvert was also given permission to raise his special unit. He called it 'Malayan Scouts (Special Air Service)'; Calvert saw in the Scouts a chance to revitalise the SAS within the Regular Army.

Initially Calvert collected together 100 volunteers at the new regiment's base in Johore. Among them were former members of Ferret Force, Force 136 and SOE, the Chindits, the wartime SAS, and even some French Foreign Legion deserters from Indo-China, as well as volunteers from many different units of the services then in Malaya. Short on manpower, Calvert signalled London for a squadron from 21 SAS; and in January 1951 Maj. Greville-Bell's 'M' Sqn. was sent to Malaya. Returning to Hong Kong, Calvert recruited Chinese interpreters and more former Chindits to assist his intelligence-gathering. From there he travelled to Southern Rhodesia to meet Rhodesian former members of the wartime British SAS, selecting a small number of volunteers from some 1,000 applicants. The original first 100 volunteers formed 'A' Sqn. of the new regiment; 'M' Sqn., 21 SAS became the basis for the Malayan Scouts' 'B' Sqn.; and the Rhodesians became 'C' Sqn.

The early days of the unit were somewhat haphazard, and many veterans recall them with pain. The original complement of the Malayan Scouts developed a name for indiscipline; happily, time and training changed this situation.

'A' Sqn. operated in the Ipoh region while 'B' and 'C' trained in Johore. Calvert's ideas were central to the training and operational methods of the unit. One of the jungle training exercises involved two soldiers stalking each other through thick undergrowth armed with airguns, and protected only by bayonet-fencing masks! Inflatable dinghies for river operations were obtained from the US Forces, and Calvert pioneered techniques for air-supplying troops in thick jungle by means of Royal Navy and RAF helicopters. He also advanced his 'hearts and minds' programme among the native tribes by setting up medical units to travel to native villages. His men learnt to live and work with the tribesmen, and with the aid of the Iban trackers they became expert at jungle fieldcraft.

Hard work and illness took their toll, and late in 1951 Calvert was invalided back to Britain a very sick man. His place was taken by Lt. Col. John Sloane, an officer recently returned from Korea, who knocked some discipline into the Malay Scouts. Under his leadership they operated in a peripheral jungle infantry rôle with the Field Force Police. In February 1952 the Scouts operated on the Thai-Malay border with the Field Force Police, Gurkhas, and Royal Marine Commando personnel. For the first time they tried out the new technique of 'tree-jumping', subsequently used successfully throughout the Malayan Emergency. This involved parachuting into tall trees, allowing the canopy to snag on the upper branches; the jumper then cut himself free and lowered himself to the ground on a rope.

In the spring of 1952 one of Calvert's original officers, Maj. John Woodhouse, was sent to Britain to set up a selection and training scheme. In 1952 the Malayan Scouts became 22nd Special Air Service Regiment, being raised under the original Corps Warrant granted to 21 SAS; the latter thus became the first Territorial Army regiment ever to 'give birth' to a Regular regiment.

22nd SAS Regiment

22 SAS inherited from the Malayan Scouts (SAS) four squadrons and an HQ establishment. During 1952 they managed to recruit from Fijian troops with whom they worked. During this and subsequent periods of service in Malaya they

An SAS unit photographed in Malaysia during the 1960s, wearing No. 7 Dress ('Warm Weather Working'). Note temporarily attached shoulder wings; small-size white rank chevrons; and black insignia on officer's shoulderstraps (centre front). (22 SAS)

formed a close bond with 55 Coy., Royal Army Service Corps, who, with the RAF, supplied the SAS when on operations.

It was also in autumn 1952 that John Woodhouse 'set up shop' at the Airborne Forces Depot, Aldershot, home of the Parachute Regiment; here he recruited and trained volunteers from the Regular Army for the SAS in Malaya. In those early days some animosity was felt between SAS and Airborne Forces. Due to the superficial fact that the SAS still wore the 'cherry beret' and titles in Airborne Forces colours, some felt that they should be subject to Airborne Forces HQ, and less independent.

SAS action against the Malayan CTs continued, with some innovations. The Iban trackers were now formed into their own unit, The Sarawak Rangers. The experience of the SAS in jungle encounters led to the testing of different types of shotgun and shotgun load; for Close Quarter Battle (CQB), the Browning semi-automatic 12-gauge was found satisfactory. The Malayan jungle war helped the SAS to develop a wide range of skills which are now part of SAS training. Among the most obvious was the emphasis placed on mastering the language and regional dialects of the area of operations. A sound basis of medical skill was also written into the programme: essential not only for the safety of the isolated SAS patrol, but also for furthering the 'hearts and minds' policy among the local natives begun by Mike Calvert and continued and developed after his

departure. The SAS contact drills evolved b small patrols, instilling an instinctive reaction to contact with an enemy ahead, behind or on either flank, became a 'blueprint' for special force operations; they differ markedly from regular infantry platoon work, and have added several innovations to the British Army infantry textbook Emphasis was also placed on signals skills; the signaller among the team paid for his expertise by having to haul a 30lb radio and spares as well as a heavy Bergen rucksack.

In 1955 Woodhouse returned from Britain and arranged for a new squadron to be included in 22 SAS: the Parachute Squadron, led by Maj Dudley Coventry, was drawn from the three Regular battalions of the Parachute Regiment The Rhodesians of 'C' Sqn., having now completed three years, returned to Rhodesia. They were replaced by other Commonwealth forces late in 1955 an Independent New Zealand Squadron arrived. The decision had been taken the previous year by the NZ Government, and a call for volunteers allowed selection of 138 from 800 civilian applicants, and 40 officers and NCOs A third of the personnel were Maoris.

By 1956 22 SAS had a strength of 560 all rank in 'A', 'B', 'D', NZ, and Para Squadrons, and the HQ element. That year they were visited by the Prime Minister, Harold Macmillan; this unusua show of interest was due to the political desirability of a well-publicised British military success in Malaya following the abortive Suez operation o that year. On this occasion 22 SAS put on a magnificent display of their skills at Johore, in addition to turning out a guard of honour which would have done credit to the Brigade of Guards.

One skill which the SAS had developed to a fine art at about this time was exiting from helicopters In heavy jungle it was not always possible for the choppers to land, and the SAS evolved technique for 'abseiling' down ropes, or even parachuting from the helicopters at low level.

The year 1957 brought sweeping changes to the British Army. This was the period of amalgamations and disbandments, of the end of National Service, of new weapons and equipment. In July 1957 22 SAS was cut down to two squadrons and an HQ. The final connection with Airborne Forces was severed, and the Parachute Squadron

Early 1960s: members of 22 SAS, wearing 'woolly pullies' and regimental stable belts, attend a lecture on US small arms from a 'Green Beret' NCO at Fort Bragg, N. Carolina. (22 SAS)

was removed from 22 SAS and returned to Airborne Forces control. The SAS now reverted to the beige beret. In November/December the New Zealand Squadron returned home and was disbanded. One of the British Squadrons was also disbanded and its personnel distributed between the other two.

By the end of 1957 the Malayan terrorist campaign was virtually over. Malaya had ceased to be a Crown colony at the end of August that year. The SAS, who had accounted for 108 CTs during their time in Malaya, now undertook deep jungle penetration missions in search of the last pockets of resistance.[1]

Oman: Dhofar and the Jebel

The ancient sultanate of Muscat and Oman, at the extreme eastern tip of the Arabian peninsula, was in the throes of rebellion in 1958. The medieval rule of the sultan was threatened by a group of Omani noblemen and their followers, backed by American oil interests and by the neighbouring Saudi Arabian monarchy. By 1958 the rebellion was four years old, and the rebels were operating with some freedom from a plateau, Jebel Akhdar (Green Mountain), in the Dhofar mountains. Britain had a limited commitment to the sultan in that British officers were supplied to train his army of Baluchi mercenaries from Pakistan and Afghanistan. In July 1957 the British Government publicly ruled out any large-scale posting of British troops to Oman; but it was clear that without British intervention the rebels were never going to be cleared from their 8,000ft.-high refuge.

The commander of the sultan's forces was Lt.Col. David Smiley; when his request for British troops met with a refusal to commit more than two battalions, he asked that one of them be either a parachute battalion, a Royal Marine Commando, or an SAS unit. In the event the Life Guards, the Trucial Omani Scouts, and REME and Royal Signals support were sent to the sultanate. Following a meeting in Oman between an expert in guerilla warfare, Maj. Frank Kitson, and the new CO of 22 SAS, Lt.Col. Anthony Deane-Drummond, arrangements were made for the

SAS soldiers in the type of camouflaged 'windproof' worn in the 1970s before the introduction of DPM camouflage material. (21 SAS)

transfer of a squadron of 22 SAS from Malaya to Oman in November 1958. They were followed in December by the other squadron and the HQ establishment. Working mainly at night, they soon gained a foothold on the Jebel Akhdar. Working in co-ordination with the other units mentioned, 22 SAS overran the Jebel in January 1959, and drove the rebels off. The lesson that 22 SAS could succeed where conventional forces failed, in desert as well as jungle, was not lost on Whitehall. The 22nd Special Air Service Regiment was recalled to Britain, for the first time since their formation.

Consolidation and Co-operation

A period of consolidation now followed, while the Army completed the reforms decreed in 1957. 22 SAS was headquartered at Malvern in Worcestershire for a short time, moving to Bradbury Lines barracks at Hereford in 1960.

In 1959 a third SAS regiment came into being, 23rd Special Air Service Regiment (Volunteers), initially launched at Finsbury Barracks in North London, and shortly thereafter moved to Solihull, Birmingham. It was formed initially from the Reserve Reconnaissance Unit, whose function had been to develop and teach methods of escape and evasion; the RRU was the successor to MI9, the wartime department responsible for similar activities in aid of shot-down RAF airmen behind

[1] Not including those killed by the Malayan Scouts (SAS) before 1952.

The first SAS patrol Land Rovers in the early 1960s were armed with the same weapons as the wartime jeeps—Brens, .50cal. Brownings, Vickers K mountings. (22 SAS)

enemy lines. After their return to Britain 22 SAS both liaised with and trained the two TA regiments, passing on knowledge and skills; 21 and 23 SAS also profited by picking up some former members of the Malayan Scouts (SAS) and 22 SAS after they left the Regular Army. During 1960 one squadron of 22 SAS carried out operational training in East Africa.

During the period of relative inactivity in Britain, the SAS concept was bearing fruit overseas, and contact was maintained with friendly counterparts. In July 1957 the 1st SAS Company was formed at Swanbourne Barracks, Western Australia; and a reserve SAS formation was created as part of the Citizen Military Force from 1st Bn., City of Sydney's Own Regt. (Commando). The end of the Malayan Emergency removed the immediate reason for their existence; but in 1960 the SAS Company became part of the Royal Australian Regiment, taking on the mantle of commando and special forces work within the Australian forces.

In December 1959 the NZ Army HQ approved the re-activation at troop strength of the New Zealand SAS, and early in 1960 this unit was expanded to a squadron. Training had been carried out in conjunction with the Australian SAS. In 1961 a territorial unit was added to the strength of the regular NZSAS squadron. A rôle emerged for both Australian SAS and NZSAS within the South East Asian Treaty Organization: defence of the homeland through defence of its approaches. Since the 'approaches' in both cases

consist of jungle terrain, the two units developed their skills in terms of jungle LRRPs (long-range reconnaissance patrols) and behind-the-line sabotage, training in the jungles of New Guinea.

At this period there was a certain measure of liaison between 22 SAS and the US Army's Special Forces. The first SF Group had been formed in 1952; and by 1960 a parent body in the form of 1st Special Forces, with the 1st, 7th and 10th SF Groups under command, operated from the Special Warfare Center at Fort Bragg, North Carolina. At this stage the 'Green Berets' were enjoying very positive support and encouragement from President John F. Kennedy.

From this point on there was a degree of cross-training between the US Special Forces and the SAS, both British and Commonwealth. The SF were at this time already operating in Vietnam as advisers to ARVN units. They drew to some extent upon SAS experience, developing their own techniques and 'hearts and minds' programmes in several South American states. However, there were differences in approach. The basic US SFG units were a 'B' team of 23 men commanding anything from four to 12 four-man 'A' teams, all cross-specialised, whereas the basic SAS unit was the four-man patrol.

In 1961, 'C' Sqn.—the old Rhodesian unit from Malayan days—was re-activated at Ndola in Northern Rhodesia (now Zambia) as part of the forces of the Federation of Rhodesia and Nyasaland, with 250 all ranks. A volunteer contingent of officers and NCOs trained with 22 SAS at Bradbury Lines. The same year saw formation of a Danish unit directly inspired by the British SAS entitled the *Jaegerkorpset*. In May 1962 Norway also formed an SAS-type unit of *Jeger* Patrols. Both these countries' troops were regular training-fellows of 21 SAS. The Artists moved barracks in 1962 from Euston down to the Duke of York's HQ in King's Road, Chelsea.

May 1962 also saw a 30-man detachment of the NZSAS Sqn. flown to Thailand to work with the US Army. At that time SEATO feared a Chinese-backed guerilla war on Thailand's north-east border. The NZ detachment was split between Udon, where they worked with US 'Green Berets' and Marines, and Khao, where they trained Thai personnel alongside US Army Rangers. The

NZSAS contingent was withdrawn when the threat receded in September 1962. At roughly this time Australian SAS troops are known to have been deployed in Thailand, primarily on training exercises.

Back at Hereford, 22 SAS were training the 'Special Reconnaissance Squadron'. SRS was formed in 1962 from volunteers drawn from Royal Armoured Corps regiments, and was intended to operate in an SAS-type rôle in Germany. This is perhaps the logical point to record that in 1964 the SRS was brought back to Britain and amalgamated with 'C' Sqn., 2nd Royal Tank Regt.—'Cyclops'—a parachute unit. In February 1965 the amalgamated unit was renamed 'Royal Armoured Corps Parachute Squadron'.

Late in 1962 Lt.Gen. Sir Charles Richardson, Director General of Military Training, visited SAS units working with the US Special Forces in the USA. At Fort Bragg he saw SAS men studying advanced demolitions and advanced field medicine techniques, training with a wide range of foreign weapons, and studying new languages. General Richardson was greatly impressed by what he saw, and reported in such favourable terms on the motivation and skills of the SAS that the attitude of the British military establishment towards the regiment improved, and the SAS was re-equipped and modernised. Up to that point they had suffered from the inevitable reaction of all conventional establishments to 'private armies': that they were mavericks and parasites, creaming off the best men from other regiments, and wasting resources better employed elsewhere. At that time it was generally believed that a tour with the SAS was one of the surest ways to ruin one's Army career. The improved climate came just in time: SAS were about to be committed to another war.

Borneo and Aden

In December 1962 Communist guerillas, supported by the Indonesian dictator Sukarno, started a rebellion in the British dependency of Borneo. Sukarno was seeking to expand Indonesian influence, by coercion and force if need be, over the other islands in the region. Col. Woodhouse immediately set out to convince the Ministry of Defence of the desirability of an SAS presence. The initial rebellion was put down by an airlift of

The Brownings later replaced the lighter weapons; and GPMGs finally replaced the Brownings. The operations carried out in the Arabian Gulf area led to the adoption of a dark pink camouflage paint which proved most effective in the desert, and the Land Rovers were quickly dubbed 'Pink Panthers'. (22 SAS)

Gurkhas, Queen's Own Highlanders and 42 Cdo. RM from Singapore, but the threat of Indonesian infiltration was unabated.[1] In Borneo the senior British officer, Maj.Gen. Sir Walter Walker, head of the Brigade of Gurkhas, enthusiastically welcomed the idea of deploying SAS troops in an intelligence-gathering and LRRP rôle. In 1963 the Malaysian Federation, including part of Borneo, was proclaimed, and Sukarno announced his intention of destabilising the young state. In January one squadron of 22 SAS arrived in Borneo and promptly renewed contacts with their old friends from Malayan days, the Iban trackers. Another arrived in April after completing a period of winter training in Germany and Norway.

In mid-1963 units of 22 SAS and 'C' (Rhodesian) Sqn. SAS trained together in Aden. Soon after the 'C' Sqn. men returned home the break-up of the Federation of Rhodesia and Nyasaland led them to pack up and move from Ndola to new barracks at Cranborne.

In New Zealand the centenary of the formation of two famous local guerilla units of the Maori Wars, the Forest Rangers and the Taranaki Bush Rangers, led to the renaming of the NZSAS, which became 1st Ranger Sqn., NZSAS.

Both the Gurkha Independent Parachute Coy.

---

[1] HQ 3 Cdo. Bde. RM, 40 Cdo. RM and other units from this brigade, including the SBS, served in the countries of Borneo from 1962 to 1966.

and the Guards Independent Parachute Coy. were committed to Borneo. The Gurkha IPC was used to train a unit called the Border Scouts, but both the Independent Coys. were later trained as Special Reconnaissance Units. That the SAS were thin on the ground became obvious. An HQ complement was sent out from the UK and set up on Labuan Island in Brunei. Permission was received to raise a new squadron in 22 SAS, and officers toured BAOR units for recruits; others came from troops already serving on the island, including a battery from 95 Cdo. Regt. RA serving in 3 Cdo. Bde. RM.

Enemy activity in December 1963 confirmed that Indonesian regulars were crossing the border. The SAS four-man patrols were monitoring infiltration, living with the natives and following a 'hearts and minds' policy which gained local support. Normally the patrol would move in the order: lead scout, patrol commander, signaller, and medic. The last man usually carried a 7.62mm GPMG or Bren, the remainder a mixture of 5.56mm M16 Armalite rifles and SLRs. The pump-action shotgun was also available if occasion demanded. January 1964 saw one squadron allocated an operational area in the Third Division Mountains along the Brunei-Indonesia frontier, and here they periodically saw action against infiltrators.

Thousands of miles west and north, another trouble-spot was simmering. Aden had been a British colony since 1939. Lying at the tip of the Arabian peninsula, this unlovely spot guards the southern entrance to the Red Sea and thus the Suez Canal; in the early 1960s it was divided into the Federation in the south-west and the Protectorate in the north-east. President Nasser of Egypt, and behind him his Russian allies, looked greedily at this strategic colony. In September 1962 the ruler of the Yemen, north of Aden, was ousted by an army coup engineered by Egypt. Supporters of the leader gathered in the mountains on the Yemeni-Aden border, and were joined by mercenaries, some of them former SAS men. In late 1963, with the British already engaged in a jungle war in Borneo, the time looked ripe for the Egyptians, the Yemenis and their Russian paymasters to foment disorder in Aden. Initially they armed and supplied hill tribes in the Jebel Radfan

mountains, and provided them with instructors. Federal Regular Army (Aden) troops, with British assistance, failed to dislodge the insurgents.

At that time a squadron of 22 SAS was on a rest period at Hereford, and in early 1964 its CO visited Aden to organize a repetition of the training carried out there with the Rhodesians the previous year. He suggested that the squadron could be brought out in advance of its training date, and used operationally. MOD approval quickly brought the squadron out to Aden, where they formed part of 'Radforce', a command assembled to storm the Jebel Radfan and seize it from the insurgents. 'Radforce' consisted of 45 RM Cdo. with 'B' Coy., 3rd Bn., Parachute Regt. attached; a Royal Tank Regt. squadron; a Royal Horse Artillery battery, and a Royal Engineers troop. To this force were added two FRA battalions, and the SAS squadron. At the end of April 1964 'Radforce' went on the offensive.

The plan called for the seizure of two central Radfan hill positions, one by the Commandos and the other by the Paras. Members of the SAS squadron would be inserted by night to mark out and secure two DZs for the paratroopers. As ill-luck would have it the SAS party was accidentally discovered, and surrounded by tribesmen. Air and artillery support allowed the party to extract itself in a fierce firefight, but they lost the patrol commander and signaller, whose bodies were later beheaded and displayed by the hillmen. Their deaths caused a stir in Britain, not only because of the distressing circumstances, but also because their families had been under the impression that this squadron was exercising on Salisbury Plain. In May 1964 the squadron returned to the UK before redeploying to Borneo. For the next two years this would be a common pattern, with the SAS fighting a jungle war in Borneo and a desert war in Aden, by rotation: it was known in the regiment as the 'Happy Time'.

Back in Borneo, mid-1964 saw the mounting of an offensive, with SAS troops leading cross-border raids against the Indonesians; initially limited to penetrations of 5,000 yards, these were later increased to 20,000 yards. Field artillery would 'soften up' an area, and then infantry led by the SAS would make a lightning 'shoot 'n scoop' raid and withdraw. In preparation for these raids the

1. Captain, 'L' Detachment SAS; North Africa, 1942
2. Sergeant, 'L' Detachment; North Africa, 1941
3. Major David Stirling, North Africa, 1942

A

1. Lieutenant, 2nd SAS; NW Europe, 1944–45
2. Corporal, SAS; Aegean, 1943
3. Sergeant, 3rd (French) SAS; NW Europe, 1945

B

1. Private, French Demi-Brigade SAS; Indo-China, 1946
2. Trooper, Australian SAS; South Vietnam, 1970
3. Trooper, Rhodesian SAS, 1979

C

1. Corporal, 21 SAS, 1948–49
2. Captain, 21 SAS; No. 1 Dress, 1953
3. Trooper, 21 SAS, 1960

D

1. Officer, 22 SAS; Malaya, 1953
2. Sergeant, 22 SAS, No. 3 Dress; Malaya, c.1956
3. Trooper, 22 SAS; Oman, 1970

E

1. Trooper, 22 SAS; HALO rig, 1980
2. Major, 22 SAS; No. 2 Dress, 1980
3. Staff Sergeant, 22 SAS; barrack dress, 1980

F

1. Major, 21 SAS; No. 1 Dress, 1980
2. Corporal, 21 SAS; No. 2 Dress, 1980
3. Trooper, 23 SAS; combat dress, 1980

G

1. Swimmer/Canoeist, RMS BS, 1980
2. Staff Sergeant, RMS BS, Lovat Dress, 1980
3. SAS trooper, Iranian Embassy, 1980

H

SAS carried out cross-border recce patrols. Besides the SAS, members of the 3 Cdo. Bde. RM Special Boat Section were also operating in Borneo in four-man patrols.

In September 1964 the Australian SAS Company was removed from the RAR and expanded into the Australian Special Air Service Regiment; it now comprised an HQ and Base Squadron, 1 and 2 Sabre Squadrons, and a Signals Squadron (151). White-on-red 'Special Air Service' shoulder titles were worn; the beige beret bore a black cloth shield with a metal winged dagger cap badge. (The Rhodesians adopted the same arrangement; at this time the NZSAS still retained the maroon beret and the embroidered cloth SAS badge.) Late in 1964 both Australia and New Zealand, as members of SEATO and the Commonwealth, authorised the deployment of their SAS troops in Borneo.

In 1964 the Rhodesian Front government of Ian Smith declared UDI—'unilateral declaration of independence'—from Britain. For the next 15 years the Rhodesian SAS would have no official links with its sister units; it is sad to speculate what might have happened if, in the early days of UDI, it had been forced to fight against a British attempt to restore legality by military means. But Britain had its hands full in Aden and Borneo.

At this time SAS staff were among those passing on the skills learnt in Borneo at the SEATO Jungle Warfare Training Centre at Kota-Tingi in Malaya. Unconfirmed rumours suggested that ARVN, South Korean and American units received training there prior to operations in Vietnam. Among the concepts taught at Kota-Tingi was the use of tracker dogs, which may have prompted the US Army in Vietnam to form its K9 units.

In February 1965, 1 Sqn., Australian SAS and 1 Detachment, 1st Ranger Sqn., NZSAS arrived in Brunei; based at Kuching, they received preliminary training at Tutang. Other reinforcements for the SAS at this time came from 'C' Coy., 2nd Bn., Parachute Regt., trained and deployed by the SAS as a Special Reconnaissance Unit. As the year drew on Indonesian offensive action slackened; they began to withdraw, abandoning their jungle HQs and support bases. Simultaneously, things were heating up in Aden, where the regiment had enjoyed a number of successes 'up-country'.

To combat increased urban terrorism against all forms of British presence by the Russian-backed NLF and the Egyptian-backed FLOSY organizations, a special squad was formed from members of the SAS squadron on Aden duty. The 'Keeni-Meeni' or 'K-M' Squad took its name from a Swahili word describing the stalking movements of a snake. Between 1965 and the British withdrawal from Aden, 'K-M' squads in Arab dress killed and captured many would-be bombers and assassins. The task became more perilous when other British Army and police units tried their hand at the same tactics.

March 1966 saw the decline of Sukarno and the tailing-off of the war in Borneo; by the end of the year even mopping-up operations had ceased. That year, 22 SAS were increased by the addition of a squadron drawn from Brigade of Guards recruits. In November the Australian and New Zealand SAS left Borneo. The 1st Australian SAS Regt. was increased by a third squadron, immediately committed to Vietnam.

Back in Aden a third front opened up. Communist insurgents supplied the Dhofari tribesmen on the Aden-Oman border with weapons and assistance to fight the British. The Irish Guards and a squadron of 22 SAS were sent to the area; a classically conventional and ponderous infantry attack on the Dhofari camps allowed many rebels to escape, however. The war in Aden closed with the planned British withdrawal of November 1967; in the face of this political abdication of responsibility the Russian and Egyptian 'advisers' were quick to step in to 'assist' the new government.

The SAS, no longer needed in Aden or Borneo, returned to Hereford.

Vietnam

Australian involvement in the Vietnam War began when, in August 1965, a 30-man training team including SAS personnel was attached to the ARVN. The first Australian-run Civilian Irregular Defence Group was set up near Quang Nai. Following Australian withdrawal from Borneo in November 1966, the new 3 Sabre Sqn., Australian SAS was sent to Vietnam as a support and recce unit for 5th Bn., Royal Australian Regiment. Further squadrons served in Vietnam by rotation. They established an operational area in Phuoc Tuy province south-east of Saigon, with a base at Nui Dat.

For obvious logistic reasons the Australian SAS in Vietnam used US Special Forces equipment rather than British. They expanded the four-man patrol concept by adding a second-in-command, and were able to employ much of the jungle skill learned in Borneo. They were very effective in LRRP operations; and the US Supreme Commander, Gen. Westmoreland, ordered the formation of LRRP/Recondo teams along SAS lines by all US infantry brigades. In November 1968, 4 Troop, 1st Ranger Sqn., NZSAS joined the Australians at Nui Dat.

The Australian and New Zealand experience in Vietnam was generally unhappy. Among the most effective troops in the country, they found that their proven methods were not always in line with current US thinking. To a large extent the US Army fought the war with technology, and even the movements of light striking forces were heavy and clumsy by SAS standards. Excellent relations were built up with ARVN Rangers, US Special Forces and ROK 'Tiger' units, however. With Australasian disengagement from Vietnam both Australian and New Zealand SAS personnel left the country in February 1971.

It has been claimed by certain elements of the media that British SAS men fought and even died in Vietnam. The official response of all parties involved has been an outright denial. It has been suggested that British SAS men might have reached Vietnam through secondment or exchange programmes with the US Special Forces or the Australian SAS. It could equally be true, of course, that US 'Green Berets' on a similar programme at Bradbury Lines might have slipped

The basic four-man SAS patrol—leader, scout, medic and signaller; hot weather combat kit is worn here. The weapons are the Armalite rifle and a pump-action 12-bore shotgun. The medic's kit is laid out in this posed photo. (22 SAS)

off for operational duty in Borneo. The committed propagandist can seize on any supposition and give it a tinge of credibility: given the natural and necessary links between the special forces of the free world, one could advance the idea of Australasian SAS men or US 'Green Berets' seeing service in Oman, or even in Ulster. All that can be said with certainty is that there is no evidence to disprove the official denials of SAS Group.

Northern Ireland and Oman

After the close of hostilities in Borneo and Aden, 22 SAS underwent a period of intense training and up-dating, and links with the TA regiments, 21 and 23 SAS, were strengthened. In the autumn of 1969, 22 SAS became involved for the first time in the centuries-old conflict which divides Ireland. The festering suspicion between the Catholic minority and the Protestant majority in Ulster—terms with more political than purely religious significance—broke into the open with serious rioting in August 1969. Both communities behaved badly, and when law and order completely broke down the British Army was called in to police the situation—initially, at the request of the Catholic civil rights leaders, who accused the Protestant authorities of serious discrimination. Both camps started to stock-pile weapons; the situation was further confused by a split in the Irish Republican Army movement between the Marxist 'Officials' and the more traditionally Republican 'Provisionals'.

In autumn 1969 Army raids on the Catholic areas of Belfast uncovered massive caches of arms and ammunition: similar action in Protestant areas, where similar caches were known to exist, was blocked by the Unionist politicians who at that time still ruled the province. The Protestant para-military counterpart to the IRA, the Ulster Volunteer Force, had been revived, and British intelligence was aware of large-scale arms buying (by both sides) in Britain and on the Continent.

Elements of 22 SAS were despatched to Ulster and based in the staunchly Protestant area of East Down. Patrolling an area from the Glens of Antrim in the north to the Mountains of Mourne in the south, along the coast, and even including searches of vessels in the east coast ports, the squadron probably acted as a deterrent to arms smuggling; at all events, no weapons were found.

In December 1969 it was reported that 200 SAS troops were back on the Malay-Thai border; what was not reported was that the SAS were back in Oman.

British intelligence had established that a guerilla training team backed by Iraq was operating along the Musandum Peninsula. A Royal Marines Special Boat Section inserted an SAS squadron on to the Peninsula, using Gemini inflatable boats; the operation was timely and successful.

In Western eyes the Sultan of Oman was a feudal tyrant whose rule provoked natural rebellion, which was encouraged and supplied by Oman's neighbours Aden and the Yemen, with some Iraqi involvement. Britain was getting nowhere fighting Sheikh Zaid's war for him until July 1970, when he was overthrown in a British-backed coup by his far more sophisticated and liberal son, Qabus. The SAS then mounted a 'hearts and minds' campaign unparalleled in recent years.

A medical programme was launched in the Dhofari mountains to improve the lot of the inhabitants, backed by a veterinary and agricultural programme to improve farm stock and techniques. In parallel, a concerted campaign was mounted against the guerillas, which sought either to 'turn' them or to isolate them from the villagers. The name of the operation was 'Storm'. At first Whitehall denied the presence of the SAS in Oman, and they were referred to simply as 'British Army Training Teams'.

Rebels were encouraged to defect, and the most useful were recruited by the young sultan's forces into *firqa* counter-guerilla units, led in their turn by SAS patrols. SAS personnel were put through an Arabic language course before being sent to Oman.

July 1972 saw perhaps one of the greatest moments in regimental history, when ten SAS men, aided by a small number of local soldiers, held off and defeated more than 250 guerillas in what has become known as the Battle of Mirbat. It is generally accepted that incidents such as Mirbat helped break the back of the Omani guerilla movement.

During the war in Oman only squadron

strength was committed to the region, by rotation. The real fighting ended late in 1975 when the SAS, its local teams and the Muscat Regiment assaulted guerilla positions along the Yemeni border and destroyed the guerilla presence. About a dozen SAS soldiers were killed during the conflict, and several times this number wounded; but these figures perhaps fail to convey the intensity of some of the fighting.

In 1975 the Guards Independent Parachute Coy. was disbanded, and 22 SAS picked up some of its members.

The Fight against Terrorism

Although there have been few examples as striking as Oman, it is a fact that many of the guerilla movements which have troubled the free world since 1945 have met with convincing defeat at the hands of Regular forces—a fact which the propaganda machine of the Left is at pains to conceal. Terrorism in the heart of the West, a more recent threat, requires entirely different methods. For the SAS this has meant the development of teams with specialist anti-terrorist training.

The SAS has been involved in fighting terrorism since at least 1972, when a threat was issued that the Cunard liner *Queen Elizabeth II* would be blown up unless a ransom was paid. A party comprising two members of 22 SAS Boat Troop, two members of the RM Special Boat Squadron, and a para-qualified member of the RAOC carried out a 'wet jump' in mid-Atlantic to board and search the liner. Nothing was found.

A milestone in counter-terrorist tactics was the tragic incident that September, when Palestinian terrorists kidnapped Israeli athletes at the Munich Olympics. The subsequent police ambush went wrong, and in the battle which followed five terrorists and all their hostages died. In consequence the West German government set up a specialist unit, GSG9; and in Britain the SAS was ordered to develop anti-terrorist units and strategy.

The specialist teams were formed and trained at Hereford, where the SAS created and 'replayed' every imaginable dryland hijack and hostage situation, including building takeovers and compound and aircraft seizures. Bradbury Lines has a specially-built 'CQB house' in which sophisticated techniques are tested and skills imparted. At various times during the mid- and late 1970s 'dummy runs' of considerable complexity were carried out in co-ordination with the police and other authorities; and SAS men have on several occasions been deployed to guard against threatened actions which did not, in the event, take place.

The IRA campaigns of murder and bombing on the mainland at various times during the past decade led to SAS teams being placed on alert. In December 1975 an IRA four-man active service unit, later convicted of a number of murders, was trapped by police in a flat at Balcombe Street, Marylebone with two hostages. The IRA men were informed that an SAS team was standing by, and promptly surrendered.

Back to Ireland

On 6 January 1976 the Prime Minister announced that following a rise in the level of violence the SAS were being deployed in the South Armagh border area; and a complete squadron was initially deployed. This was the first public admission that 22 SAS had entered the province.

The question of SAS deployment in Ulster is bedevilled by propaganda. The SAS has acquired a formidable reputation, and is the object of widespread paranoia in the Irish media, who see its hand behind every action of the security forces. Unlikely 'British ex-soldiers' with tales of SAS dirty tricks are periodically produced by Dublin newspapers. Phrases like 'black propaganda' and 'phantom murder gang' are bandied about in IRA jargon.

Sadly, the activities of plain-clothes patrols from other Army units have on occasion assisted this propaganda campaign. When British soldiers appeared in court charged with shooting civilians with captured IRA weapons from unmarked cars; when, in a time of sectarian car-bombings, a British soldier stole a car; then these acts of tragic incompetence or simple personal stupidity were cried up by the Republican propagandists as examples of 'the SAS committing atrocities to pin on the IRA'.

Typical SAS belt kit, basically of British '58 pattern with some US and Bundeswehr items added 'to taste'. Apart from rations, water, and SLR magazines the belt rig also accommodates compact escape/evasion survival kit and first aid kit. The SAS soldier can therefore function on operations without heavy packs and independent of support. (Terry Fincher)

In May 1974 it was admitted that 'SAS-trained soldiers' were active in Ulster. This usually means that men who had completed a three- or six-year tour with the SAS and had returned to their parent unit were now serving with that unit in the province; naturally, the skills they acquired in 22 SAS were at the disposal of their regiments.

The wild claims of previous SAS activity were shown up by the arrival and subsequent success of the SAS in 1976.

In 1977, when a map-reading error led members of 22 SAS over the unmarked border into Eire, sections of the Irish media represented the incident as proof of the activity of 'SAS murder squads' inside the Republic. The Special Criminal Court in Dublin later accepted the explanation of error and set the men free.

Royal Marine Commandos have operated frequently in Ulster, particularly in the 'bandit country' of South Armagh. It has been rumoured, but never admitted, that members of the RM SBS

have carried out SAS-type operations as part of the Commando stationed there.

The members of 22 SAS continue to serve in Ulster today.

* * *

In May 1977 the SAS assisted the Dutch Marines and police in handling a train hijack by Moluccan terrorists. The train siege ended successfully for the authorities; and, drawing upon this experience, the SAS carried out a similar exercise that autumn on a stretch of the Hereford to Worcester railway line with the co-operation of the Hereford Police and British Rail.

In October 1977 a two-man SAS team assisted

the German GSG9 unit in storming a German airliner held by hijackers at Mogadishu. There they encountered the Heckler & Koch sub-machine gun, and found it more suitable than the Ingram MAC-11 previously employed.

The Embassy Siege

On 5 May 1980 the SAS hit the headlines across the world when members of the regiment stormed the Iranian Embassy in Knightsbridge, London. Seen by millions of television viewers around the world, the operation has increased the air of mystery and (sometimes hysterical) legend surrounding the SAS; to the regiment, it was just another job.

The Territorial SAS soldier of the 1970s in old-style camouflaged windproof, drab green lightweight trousers, personally assembled belt kit, and rucksack. Note sling and swivels removed from SLR. (21 SAS)

The embassy was seized at the end of April by an obscure separatist group, to publicise their protests against the tyrannical regime of the Ayatollah Khomeini. In return for the release of the embassy staff, visiting journalists and the police constable who had been on duty outside, they demanded the release by the Iranian government of large numbers of their colleagues imprisoned in Iran. From the outset the Iranian authorities were less than helpful, and seemed not only resigned, but even eager at the prospect of the 'martyrdom' of the embassy staff.

Negotiations between the police and the terrorists initially went well, following the cautious pattern long established as the best approach to these situations. On 5 May the negotiations broke down, however; the terrorists announced their intention of murdering the hostages one by one, and began by shooting the Press Attaché and throwing his body out of the building. The situation had now reached the point of no return, and the SAS were ordered in.

The plan was for eight men to rappel down ropes from the roof at the back of the embassy, blow in the windows with 'frame charges', enter the building and kill the terrorists. Meanwhile another four men would storm the front of the building across adjoining balconies and blow their way in with another frame charge. Through a barrage of CS gas and the fire caused by their 'flash-bang' stun-grenades, the SAS stormed through the broken windows with H & K HP5 sub-machine guns, rescuing the remaining hostages and killing all but one of the terrorists. The SAS had shown an unprecedentedly large audience that it was quite capable of adjusting to the streets of London as well as to the deserts of Oman and the jungles of Malaysia.

The SAS Today

The British SAS regiments are under the overall direction of SAS Group, and currently comprise one Regular and two Territorial regiments, respectively 22, 21 and 23 SAS. Relations between the Regular and Territorial units are close, 22 SAS providing officers and senior NCOs on secondment to 21 and 23, which have squadrons based throughout the country. Soldiers in both Regular and TA units are carefully selected and given specialist training. The selection process completed by the TA SAS soldier is similar to that of his Regular counterpart, although spread over a longer period. There are three TA selection courses each year, which take about four months; they involve prolonged work-up training before a week of tests. One element of the selection process is the 'long drag', a march of approximately 36km to be completed in 20 hours, over both marsh and hill terrain, carrying 50lb of kit. Physical fitness and resistance to psychological stress are absolutely basic requirements, rigorously tested.

The skills demanded of the SAS soldier, which provide the basic four-man patrol with a degree of cross-specialisation, naturally require a high calibre of recruit. A general maturity of outlook is also essential, and the SAS has long experience in weeding out potential 'cowboys'. After selection the successful trooper then begins a process of continuation training in skills similar to those of his Regular counterpart, except, naturally enough, for the ultra-sophisticated techniques of counter-terrorist operations. The TA regiments recruit not only among recent ex-members of 22 SAS and other Regular units and by transfer from other Reserve units, but also directly from civilian life, and thus represent a broad cross-section of society.

Regular and TA SAS men are often used as the 'enemy' in military manoeuvres, and have been deployed to test security at military establishments. Alongside Parachute Regiment and Royal Marine Commando personnel, a permanent SAS staff teach their skills at a NATO LRRP school in West Germany.

The details of the strength and organization of 22 SAS are naturally restricted. In general terms it may be said that the regimental HQ controls a training wing, an administrative wing, a number of 'Sabre Squadrons', and a signals squadron. The Sabre Squadrons, which frequently operate separately and independently, each have an HQ element and a number of Troops. Each Troop is broken down into a number of four-man patrols; each patrol can draw upon a number of specialist skills—e.g. medical, signals, weapons and demolition—and linguistic ability is also encouraged. Within the regiment as a whole certain Troops specialise in certain areas of skill: airborne,

Two soldiers of 22 SAS in training; note AR15 Armalite rifle on left, SLR L1A1 on right, and belt kit. (Terry Fincher)

amphibious, mountain and 'mobile' techniques, and so forth. Mobile techniques include the use of various types of vehicle, including the well-known 'Pink Panther' or armed Land Rover.

RM Special Boat Squadron

The origins of the RMSB Sqn. lie in the complex evolution of special raiding, reconnaissance and ship-attack units formed during the Second World War. The RM Boom Patrol Detachment was one of these units; its first success was the famous limpet-mine raid on German shipping in Bordeaux in December 1942, which is popularly known as the 'Cockleshell Heroes' raid. After the war a number of amalgamations eventually gave birth to the Amphibious School RM, situated at Eastney, Portsmouth. In this Amphibious School was the 'Small Raids Wing', which later became 'Special Boat Company', and since 1977 'Special Boat Squadron'.

This organisation forms the headquarters and training unit for the operational Special Boat

Cap badge and arm patches of 21st SAS Regt. (Artists) (v)— see discussion of details under Plate D1.

Sections, which are deployed to act separately under the operational command of Commando units—3 Cdo. Bde. RM—or other commands or headquarters. Nos. 1, 2 and 3 SB Sections were Regular units, and Nos. 4 and 5 were formed from RM Reserve units. No. 6 SB Section was formed in 1952 in Malta. In December 1964 the Amphibious School, with the Special Boat Coy., moved to its present establishment at Poole, Dorset. It should be emphasised that this unit was never known as 'Special Boat Service', and should not be confused with that wartime arm of the SAS. The amphibious troop of 22 SAS, known as Boat Troop, carry on the traditions of Earl Jellicoe's wartime Special Boat Service.

Recruitment is from the ordinary ranks of the Royal Marine Commandos. Applicants go through an aptitude and fitness test, and a two-to-three-week selection test including a week's diving. This is followed by a 15-week course in seamanship, boatwork, demolition, navigation and diving. After a further four-week parachuting course the marine is passed as a Swimmer Canoeist Grade 3, and passes to an operational SB Section. Advancement to SC2 involves a three-month course in photo- and beach-reconnaissance and planning. Officers take the course as far as SC1 and then branch off into specialised courses. Unlike SAS troopers, members of RMSB Sqn. do not have to leave the unit after a set tour, although officers and senior NCOs may leave it to advance their promotion prospects.

The Royal Marines have managed to keep the rôle of RMSB Sqn. out of the public eye to a greater extent than the Army have the SAS. A blurred line separates the activities of RMSB Sqn. and SAS; it has been said that RMSB Sqn. handle all operations from high-tide mark to 12 miles inland, and SAS all other operations, but this has never been a hard and fast rule. RMSB Sqn. have been cast in the rôle of a forward beach reconnaissance, demolitions and sabotage unit, but their skills and activity extend beyond this. Besides Klepper canoes, SCs will use Gemini craft, surfboards, and insertion by submarine or Rigid Raiding Sqn. craft. They are, as mentioned, fully parachute-trained, and specialise in 'wet jumps'. As with the SAS, an RAF Special Forces servicing unit is established with the RMSB Sqn.

The Squadron has Sections, equivalent to SAS Troops, deployed with Royal Marine units throughout the world. It features prominently in manoeuvres in the Scandinavian Arctic; and since 1960 has carried out training, exchanges and exercises with the US Navy's Underwater Demolition Teams and SEALs as well as Recondo units. It has seen action in Borneo and Oman. Its rôle in the *Queen Elizabeth II* incident has been mentioned.

Royal Marine SCs do not use 'wet suits' when diving, preferring the 'dry suit', with a closed-circuit oxygen system which avoids tell-tale bubbles. They are the inventors of the 'survival vest' which is also seen in use by the Regular and Territorial SAS; made from parachute silk, this fits under the combat windproof smock and over the diving suit. It was invented because of the lack of pockets in the diving suit; its pockets hold all equipment necessary for escape, evasion and survival, to the personal choice of the wearer.

Foreign SAS Units

New Zealand

Known since April 1978 as 1 New Zealand SAS Sqn., with a separate selection and training establishment, the NZSAS Centre, this unit is based at Papakura Camp. Recruits from the Regular Army spend six months learning SAS skills following selection, and then serve three or four years before returning to their parent units; further service depends on ability and suitability for promotion. There are five Troops and an HQ. The 'cherry beret' is still worn, with cloth British-style badge; wings and badges of rank follow British styles. British SAS-style stable belts are worn with barracks dress, and blackened web belts with combat dress. British DPM combat clothing is being introduced.

Australia

Based at Campbell Barracks, Swanbourne, in Western Australia, 1st Australian SAS Regiment consists of an HQ and a Base Sqn.; 1, 2 and 3 SAS Sqns.; and 151 Sqn. (Signals). After withdrawal from Vietnam the operational task was redefined as defence of the continent of Australia itself, and there are three basic elements in the Australian SAS programme: water, desert, and freefall and climbing. Water troops are skilled assault swimmers, divers and canoeists, specialising in submarine or parachute insertion. Desert troops are divided into patrols using camels deep in the desert, and those operating in seven-man patrols using a motorcycle and two long-range Land Rovers ('Pink Panthers'). Recruits from other Regular units face a ferocious selection course, on completion of which the successful trooper receives his beige beret, worn with a metal cap badge on a black cloth shield—the maroon beret was abandoned in 1964. SAS wings of British pattern are awarded on completion of a jump course at RAAF Williamstown. The combat uniform is of US pattern; the M60 is carried instead of the NATO GPMG, and both AR-15 and SLR rifles are used.

Rhodesia/Zimbabwe

During the UDI period the Rhodesian SAS was expanded, and served on many cross-border operations; indeed, an SAS trooper was the first Rhodesian soldier killed in the guerilla war starting in 1963. 'C' Sqn. operated first on cross-border raids into Mozambique, and later inside Zambia; bridges were destroyed, guerilla camps attacked, guerilla leaders killed or captured.

Insertion was by many methods including HALO jumps, low-level jumps (as low as 450 feet) directly into the middle of the target camps, or drops further from the objective followed by cross-country approaches. In 1974 a parachute-qualified tracking and counter-guerilla unit was formed from 'C' Sqn. and named 'The Selous Scouts'. The unit worked alongside the SAS, until disbandment following charges of excessive political involvement. In June 1978 'C' Sqn. became 1 (Rhodesian) SAS Regiment; in 1979 it moved

Current pattern of SAS ('sabre') wings (top) in white, dark blue and pompadour blue thread. (Bottom) in brass, for tropical issue.

from Cranborne near Salisbury to a new purpose-built barracks named Kabrit, after the first SAS base in Egypt in 1941. At the time of writing the future of this unit under Black Majority Rule of the new state of Zimbabwe is uncertain; it is believed that many members have left, either for South Africa or to return to Britain.

Canada

In 1979 Canada unveiled its Special Service Force, which, though mainly a highly-trained light infantry unit, has some special forces capability. Members wear an arm patch of shield shape, similar to that of the Greek Ranger Raiders, and the motto 'Let Us Dare to Win'. Equipment is a mixture of British, US and West German.

The Plates

A1: Captain, 'L' Detachment SAS; North Africa, 1942
From the famous photograph of a jeep patrol. The Arab headcloth, variously known as a *keffiyah* or *shemagh* was often made from an old khaki drill shirt; it is held in place by the black goat-hair *agal*, and has tie-thongs added to the front edges so that it can be closed over the face in a sandstorm. The standard KD bush jacket has three rank 'pips' in the normal white and brown embroidery on infantry red backing on each epaulette. The SAS 'operational' parachute wings are worn on the left breast. Much personal latitude was allowed in details of dress and kit, thus the Arab sandals and tank gauntlets. Standard 1937 pattern webbing is

Four-man unit of Royal Marines SBS; a swimmer takes a limpet mine from his partner. (Royal Marines)

worn, scrubbed almost white and with dull brasses; this officer wears the pistol case, cartridge pouch and lined compass pouch, with lanyards for both pistol and compass. Many personnel carried the Fairbairn commando knife, and personal firearms were extremely various.

A2: Sergeant, 'L' Detachment SAS; North Africa, 1941
As commandos, the original personnel of 'L' Detachment generally wore standard battledress and tropical dress with the insignia of their Commando, and a wide range of headgear—Field Service caps, Scots bonnets, etc.—with the cap badges of their parent regiments. The evolution of SAS headgear and insignia are described in the body of the text; this NCO wears the short-lived white 'Chasseur' beret, and his SAS parachute wings in the 'operational' position on his breast. Rank chevrons, 1937 webbing, etc., are standard issue; the weapon is the Thompson SMG.

A3: Major David Stirling, SAS; North Africa, 1942
The founder of the SAS wears the standard khaki Service Dress cap with the cloth SAS badge sewn to the band; he and Mayne were among several officers to adopt this style, although the beret was more common. Over his battledress blouse, and the corduroy slacks so popular in the desert, Stirling wears another common expedient—a naval duffel coat or watch coat, in camel-coloured material lined with khaki denim. The crêpe-soled suede 'chukka boots' were often seen in Africa.

B1: Lieutenant, 2nd SAS; North-West Europe, 1944–45
The SAS cap badge is now worn on the maroon Airborne Forces beret. The hooded smock was worn by some personnel, others receiving the standard airborne 'Denison'. There was also some use of the battledress trousers with the enlarged 'paratrooper's' thigh pocket. Shallow puttees replace the anklets of the 1937 web set, over 'CWW' boots with cleated soles. The holster hangs low on two webbing brace attachments, and this officer favours a captured P'08 automatic as a personal sidearm. There are no visible insignia apart from the cap badge.

B2: Corporal, Special Boat Service; Aegean islands, 1943
The SAS beige beret and cloth cap badge are worn, with a heavy-knit sweater with drawstring neck; ranking is sewn to both sleeves. Standard battledress trousers are worn with bare feet and sandals. The belt, braces and basic pouches of the 1937 webbing are worn with a holster, the pistol lanyard fastened to the belt. The weapon is a captured MP.40 SMG.

B3: Sergeant, 3rd (French) SAS; North-West Europe, 1945
The less-than-complete integration of some units of the expanded SAS of 1944–45 into the identity of Stirling's original corps is suggested by this NCO's appearance on parade. The SAS cap badge is worn on the maroon beret, which is pulled left in the French manner. The so-called '1940 pattern' unpleated battledress is worn, with 1937 webbing; but instead of the correct '3rd SAS' shoulder titles in pale blue on maroon this NCO wears a short white-on-black 'France' title, as did most of his countrymen. Stiff midnight blue shoulder boards bear a silver rank chevron; and the Free French pattern of parachute wings is worn on the right breast. The 1st Airborne Division was the parent formation of the SAS Brigade, and the pale-blue-on-maroon Pegasus patch is worn on both sleeves.

A veteran of the wartime SAS recalls that the contingent of the SAS which took part in the Allied victory parade were issued with a dark blue Service Dress cap with a red band and red crown piping, adorned with a special 'bi-metal' winged sword badge in brass and silver colouring; this was worn with battledress. The rapid disbandment of the regiments prevented its becoming an established item.

C1: Private, French Demi-Brigade SAS; Indo-China, 1946

The origins and subsequent evolution of the post-war French 'SAS' units are mentioned in the narrative text. Like most of the French 5ᵉ RIC in the early days of the Indo-China war, the DBSAS were clothed and equipped from British stocks in the Far East. This *fusilier-mitrailleur* wears British tropical 'jungle greens', a lightweight shirtsleeve uniform which soon faded to a 'pea' green. It includes a bonnet similar in shape to the British General Service cap but made of the tropical material; this was popularly known in French service as the '*beret type Gurkha*' or '*type Birmanie*'. Web equipment was a chaotic mixture of British and American items; this soldier has followed a common style in fixing a pair of British 1944 pouches to his US 'pistol belt', as they conveniently held magazines for the FM.24/29 LMG. By 1950 webbing of US type had generally, but not entirely, replaced British issue.

C2: Trooper, Australian SAS; South Vietnam, 1970

US Army clothing and equipment were worn in Vietnam, for obvious reasons. The Special Forces 'tiger stripe' camouflage suit and bush-hat are worn here, with US webbing and rucksack, jungle boots, and M16 rifle. Belts of ammunition for the M60 machine gun are carried in waterproof covers.

C3: Trooper, Rhodesian SAS, 1979

The field cap with partially folded neck flap, and the shirt, are in Rhodesian camouflage material. Trousers of matching material were often replaced by drab PT shorts. Note issue boots, resembling US double-buckle type of late Second World War issue. Early shortages of clothing and equipment due to trade embargo were initially overcome with Portuguese and South African help; later a home manufacturing industry was established. The chest-rig for FN magazines is of Rhodesian make; the straps crossed behind the back, attaching to the rear of the opposite outside pouch. A British-style web belt supports two canteens of normal NATO type. Vietnam-surplus US webbing was used in quantity, and captured Eastern bloc weapons were also carried, such as the Chinese-made AKS which this trooper has taken from a fallen 'terr'; but the standard FN self-loading rifle was the norm, and was generally camouflaged—a black rifle was highly visible in the bush. The sleeves were often cut off at the shoulder for comfort on operations, or a camouflaged T-shirt substituted for the combat shirt. The only insignia are the SAS-type wings at the shoulder; these would seldom be seen in combat.

Out of the line Rhodesian SAS personnel wore standard army uniform with the lion-and-pickaxe patch on the upper arms of shirts and tunics. Beret and cap badge were of Australian style, but some soldiers acquired embroidered badges in the British style. The same stable-belt as that of the British SAS was worn.

(Top left) Current pattern of wire-embroidered SAS officer's cap badge, on dark blue patch. (Top right) Australian SAS cap badge in black shield—the Rhodesian SAS followed the same pattern. (Bottom left) The brass badge of the Greek wartime 'Sacred Squadron'. The motto is an abbreviated allusion to the classical Greek exhortation to soldiers leaving for war: 'Come back carrying your shield, or being carried on it.' This badge was worn on the right breast pocket of the shirt or BD blouse. (Bottom right) Not to be confused with British or Australian SAS insignia—the brass cap badge of the 1st Bn., Belgian Para-Commando Regt., worn on a maroon beret.

One of the sequence of pictures which caught the imagination of the world: four members of a 22 SAS counter-terrorist team frozen by the camera in the moment of storming the front of the Iranian Embassy in London on 5 May 1980. See Plate H3. (*Daily Express*)

D1: Corporal, 21 SAS, 1948–49

The first uniform of the TA regiment was wartime battledress worn open over a collar and tie, with the maroon beret bearing the white metal 'Mars and Minerva' Artists' Rifles badge. The Rifles connection was underlined by the mixed black and Rifle green lanyard, and Rifle-pattern rank chevrons—black, trimmed gold, on Rifle green. The maroon shoulder title bore in pale blue capitals '21st Special Air Service' above '(Artists)'. SAS parachute wings were awarded, and worn on the right shoulder: 'operational' breast wings could be worn only by those who had won them in wartime. The winged sword badge was worn as a sleeve patch on dark blue.

In 1949 the 'Mars and Minerva' cap badge was replaced by the winged sword badge. The two-headed motif moved down to the sleeve, being worn as a dark blue square patch with silver-grey thread embroidery. From that year the sandy yellow webbing was blackened with polish; the shoulder title changed to 'Special Air Service'; and the lanyard became all black.

Members of this unit generally preferred puttees to web anklets, perhaps for the extra ankle support given during parachute landings. They were able to obtain the distinctive SAS camouflaged smock (see Plate B1) and matching trousers, made

surplus after the disbandments of 1945; some personnel wore the Denison smock. From 1947 they were issued with Commando sweaters with drawstring necks.

D2: Captain, 21 SAS; No. 1 Dress, 1953

This ceremonial uniform was given to officers of 21 SAS for the coronation of Queen Elizabeth II in 1953, and it was later acquired by 22 SAS. The midnight blue uniform and Service Dress cap were faced with pompadour blue; the selection of the cap was to emphasise the Artists' connection with the Rifle Brigade, rather than Airborne Forces. The winged sword cap badge was in bi-metal finish, as were the smaller versions worn as 'collar dogs'. Officers below the rank of major wore trousers, and field officers cavalry-style overalls (see Plate G1), both with pompadour blue side-stripes. Rank badges and buttons were silver; woven silver cord dress epaulettes were worn. (Those worn by 22 SAS acquired a thin edging of pompadour blue piping.) Medals include the Military Cross, and wartime and post-war campaign decorations.

D3: Trooper, 21 SAS; parachuting rig, 1960

The maroon beret was finally replaced by the SAS beige beret in 1957: the cloth SAS cap badge is the only insignia worn with this uniform. Standard Denison smock, olive drab combat trousers, and blackened 1937 webbing anklets: and standard main (back pack) and reserve (chest pack) parachutes. The helmet has been embellished with a white stencil of the cap badge. The Individual Weapons Container is strapped to the right leg (when jumping from an aircraft with a port exit) and is lowered on a quick-release line as soon as the 'chute is open. It contains the trooper's weapon, disassembled to its shorter components; the container is so constructed that it can extend to take the barrels of rifles, LMGs, etc. The personal webbing kit is packed in the middle of the container.

E1: Officer, 22 SAS; Malaya, 1953

The Malayan Scouts, and the regular SAS regiment into which they evolved, started life with very little in the way of formal uniform in 1951. Jungle green fatigues (note two thigh pockets) and bush hats were worn with canvas and rubber jungle boots. Webbing equipment was mostly British 1944 pattern; this officer has the belt, canteen pockets, compass pouch (note lanyard), and pack. Apart from the jungle carbine version of the SMLE, which kicked like a mule and fired a round which was really unsuitable for the mission, many personnel carried the American .30cal. M1 carbine; this officer has magazine pouches for this weapon on his belt. Native jungle knives of various types were often added to the equipment.

In the early days of the Scouts personnel wore the insignia of their parent regiments when not 'tactical'. Those who had volunteered for the unit while already serving in the theatre often wore Malaya Command shoulder patches—a yellow kris on a green square, diagonally, with the hilt top left. The Malayan Scouts adopted their own right shoulder patch, a midnight blue shield with a white border. A white *kris* was set vertical, central, hilt up, supported by narrow up-slanting blue wings outlined white. A scroll above the motif bore 'The Malayan Scouts' in black on white; and a white 'S.A.S.' was set at the foot of the shield. Shoulder titles were worn in pale blue on maroon: 'S.A.S. Regiment' above 'Malayan Scouts'.

E2: Sergeant, 22 SAS, No. 3 Dress; Malaya, c.1956

There were two types of uniform worn for the ceremonial parades and guards of honour which the SAS often had to mount for visiting dignitaries. One was 'No. 6 Dress': khaki bush jacket and shorts, knee-length 'cherry'-coloured socks, boots GS and puttees, with the maroon beret. A black webbing belt was worn with the frog and scabbard for the SMLE's spike bayonet. The Malaya Command patches were worn on both shoulders, with SAS Para-wings on the right. Officers and senior NCOs might wear instead 'pea greens', the privately-tailored tropical jacket and trousers which were a popular if non-regulation alternative. Officers wore shoulder strap slides with their ranking and 'S.A.S.'; soldiers wore a light-and-dark-blue lanyard with their service and walking-out dress, and 'Special Air Service' shoulder titles in airborne colours. The wings worn in Malaya were based on the Second World War pattern but of local manufacture; there were tiny differences of detail, the most obvious being a line of white

stitching along the top linking the wings and the canopy.

The more formal parade uniform, illustrated here, was the 'No. 3 Dress', a white warm-weather ceremonial uniform consisting of a high-collared tunic and trousers; there seems to have been some use of webbing polished oxblood red. Rank chevrons were in gold braid, and a special gold and silver version of the para-wings was worn, both appearing on the right arm only. There were bi-metal regimental 'collar dogs', and silver buttons with the cap-badge motif. Duty NCOs wore the usual red sash over the right shoulder. Officers and senior NCOs wore black Sam Browne belts with white fittings, and black brogue shoes. This NCO wears the ribbons of the British and UNO Korean campaign medals, and the General Service ribbon for Malayan service.

'Pea-greens' were retained as unofficial tropical dress in Aden and Borneo until the late 1960s.

E3: Trooper, 22 SAS; Oman 1970

The appearance of a trooper on an extended combat mission in the desert—water was not wasted on shaving, and the local headgear of a casually-wound 'turban' was practical. The distinctive SAS camouflaged, hooded, windproof smock appeared in a number of slightly differing patterns, and a plain olive green model was occasionally seen. The windproof is worn here with a KD shirt and lightweight green trousers,

Royal Marine SBS Swimmer/Canoeist during an exercise in the Arctic. Note camouflaged Armalite, and—just visible in the original print—a set of pouches worn in a chest rig, 'Viet Cong style'. (Royal Marines)

Shoulderstrap rank slides, in black or black-green on olive green: (top) trooper, lance corporal, corporal; (bottom) sergeant, staff sergeant.

boots DMS and puttees. The 'belt kit' is issued to a standard SAS pattern, but troopers are encouraged to contrive their own preferred combinations and positions of British, US, and other foreign items.

F1: Trooper, 22 SAS; HALO rig, 1980
One of the SAS skills is 'high altitude, low opening' parachute jumping, the technique by which infiltrators leave their aircraft at a great height and free-fall, on oxygen, until safely below the enemy radar and visual surveillance. The normal parachute rig is here complicated by the addition of altimeter and oxygen equipment. The trooper's rucksack is slung upside down below the main 'chute on his back—this has been found to be the most practical position—and his GPMG is attached behind his left arm. The helmet is covered with matt tape. The SAS windproof smock and trousers are now issued in the DPM camouflage used by the rest of the Army.

F2: Major, 22 SAS, No. 2 Dress; UK, 1980
The re-introduction of the beige beret in 1957 saw the replacement not only of the airborne beret but also of the Service Dress cap; officers now wear the beret at all times with a special version of the cap badge, with silver wire wings and sword and blue scroll, all outlined red, on a shaped dark blue backing. The normal Army officer's khaki service

dress is worn, with silver regimental buttons and bi-metal 'collar dogs'. (All ranks of 22 SAS retain their own 'parent unit' service dress, simply replacing badges and buttons during their tour of duty with the SAS; it is thus possible to see examples of Guards or Highland pattern tunics, and even the occasional use of tartan trews or the kilt.) The black regimental Sam Browne and brogues are worn here; the usual SAS wings are sewn to the right shoulder, and on the breast is the General Service ribbon, indicating in this case service in the Far East and/or Arabia.

F3: Staff Sergeant, 22 SAS, Barrack Dress; UK, 1980
The regimental beret is worn with the reinforced 'woolly pully', green lightweight trousers, boots DMS and puttees, and the regimental stable belt. The ranking—a crown over three chevrons over 'S.A.S.'—appears in black on the shoulder strap slides. SAS para-wings are temporarily pinned to the right shoulder. This same uniform, with pullover or shirtsleeves, and barrack or No. 2 Dress trousers, is normally worn by officers.

G1: Major, 21 SAS, No. 1 Dress; UK, 1980
The ceremonial 'blues' are now very seldom seen in practice. Note that this uniform is almost identical to that of Plate D2, apart from the plain blue shoulder straps. As a field-rank officer he wears tight cavalry-style overalls strapped under the boots. The beret is now worn in place of the peaked cap; the black Artists' Rifles 'cartridge belt', supporting a small leather pouch at the rear, has silver whistle fittings which include a lion-mask and the wreathed Mars and Minerva badge of the regiment. This is worn with the 'blues' by the regimental CO and the 'officer of the day'. His service medals indicate East Africa and one other theatre of operations, with the bronze oakleaf of a Mention in Despatches.

G2: Corporal, 21 SAS, No. 2 Dress; UK, 1980
This NCO wears standard khaki service uniform with bi-metal 'collar dogs', regimental buttons, SAS para-wings and Artists' Rifles chevrons; the beige beret and embroidered cap badge; blackened 1937 web belt with bright brasses; and polished boots DMS. Many personnel in the Territorial SAS regiments do not apply for No. 2

Dress uniforms, as they have very few opportunities to wear them. The para-wings worn by 23 SAS are slightly different from those of 21 and 22, being slightly down-turned.

G3: Trooper, 23 SAS, combat dress; UK, 1980
The cap and windproof are made in the Army's standard DPM camouflage material. The latter has four large, loose pockets closed by large plastic buttons, a frontal zip covered by a 'velcro'd' flap, and a hood, here rolled up behind the neck: the drawstring around the bottom of the smock gives a baggy appearance. The camouflaged net face veil is worn as a scarf. The green lightweight trousers are worn, with combat boots laced with green nylon para-cord. The belt kit is typical. The SLR is coloured in green and brown camouflage stripes, and has had the sling and swivels removed; the rucksack is also streaked with brown paint.

H1: Swimmer Canoeist, Royal Marines Special Boat Squadron, 1980
The smock and trousers are in standard DPM camouflage; the belt kit is similar to that of the SAS. Black canvas and rubber boots are worn, laced partly through eyelets and partly through brass hooks. The old-style Bergen rucksack is used as a seat in the canoe. The weapon is the silenced Sterling SMG, which is also used by the SAS.

H2: Staff Sergeant, RMSB Sqn., Lovat Dress; UK 1980
The Royal Marines' 'Lovat' uniform, named after the wartime commando leader Lord Lovat and equivalent to the Army's No. 2 Dress, bears matt black buttons, 'RM' shoulder strap insignia, and 'collar dogs' in the form of the RM globe-and-laurel cap badge. Note slight differences of cut from Army No. 2 Dress. It is worn with the green commando beret with gold-coloured badge; black shoes; light khaki shirt and brown tie; and, here, the red 'duty NCO' sash. On the right sleeve are special RM para-wings, here in gold and silver on green; and on the forearm a black cloth 'tomb-

Remembrance Day parade—a misty November morning at Bradbury Lines, with wreaths laid on the clock tower on which the names of the SAS dead are recorded. (22 SAS)

stone' patch with a gold crown, 'SC' and laurel branches. (Officers do not wear these qualification patches.) The gold rank insignia appear on green backing on both sleeves.

H3: SAS Trooper; Iranian Embassy, London, May 1980

The current Army respirator was worn with a grey anti-flash hood; two-way communications equipment was carried. Over the tightly-fitting black combat clothing a black-covered 'flak' vest was worn; high patrol boots and black 'Northern Ireland' gloves completed the visible clothing. The blackened belt supported a set of magazine pouches for the H & K HP5A3 sub-machine gun (30-round 'banana' magazines), and a respirator case or other pouch containing such additional items as the magnesium-based 'stun grenades'. Photographs suggest that some at least also wore 9mm automatic pistols in open-top holsters on the right side of the belt. The trooper carries a 'frame charge' for blowing in windows.

Notes sur les planches en couleur

A1 Mélange de tenue d'uniforme et d'articles arabes; une certaine individualité était permise dans l'habillement. Brevet de parachutisme style SAS sur la poitrine. **A2** Le béret de chasseur blanc, utilisé brièvement, porté ici avec le 'battledress'. **A3** Casquette d'officier avec badge du régiment. Le duffle-coat, le pantalon de velours à côtes et les chaussures de daim étaient des articles populaires, bien qu'unofficiels, pour le désert.

B1 Badge SAS porté sur béret marron Airborne Forces. La blouse de camouflage à capuchon était portée par certains personnels, les autres recevant la blouse de parachutiste 'Denison'. Les pantalons avec poche à la cuisse de grand modèle étaient distribués par Airborne Forces. **B2** On accordait une grande latitude personnelle dans l'habillement et l'armement; notez le béret finalement choisi pour les SAS, beige pâle. **B3** Un mélange d'insignes britanniques et français est présenté ici.

C1 Uniforme de tropique britannique, comprenant le béret type 'Gurkha' et un mélange de harnachements américains et britanniques. Les grands cartouchieres britanniques étaient souvent gardées après la distribution d'équipement américain, parce qu'on pouvait y placer exactement les magasins de la mitrailleuse FM 24/29. **C2** Pour des raisons pratiques des SAS australiens au Viet Nam avaient des uniformes et équipement de l'armée américaine. **C3** Uniforme de camouflage, casquette, et cartouchieres 'type Négrier' de fabrication rhodésienne.

D1 L'uniforme de ce bataillon de parachutistes de réserve combine le modèle traditionnel des troupes de parachutistes (béret marron); les Rifles (galons noirs et verts); et le régiment traditionnel dont il provient (le badge Mars et Minerve des Artists' Rifles). **D2** L'uniforme de cérémonie fut introduit pour le couronnement de la reine Elizabeth. **D3** Le béret beige remplaça finalement le béret marron en 1957. Blouse normale 'Denison' de parachutiste; harnais noirci d'après la tradition du régiment. Les armes étaient portées dans le paquetage en dessous du parachute ventral de réserve.

E1 Uniforme règlementaire tropical; harnais de modèle 1944; carabine américaine M1, et notez le couteau de jungle indigène ajouté à l'équipement. **E2** Uniforme tropical de cérémonie blanc, toujours porté avec le béret marron; la ceinture nous permet d'identifier le sergent d'ordonnance. **E3** La blouse à capuchon de camouflage SAS 'windproof' est portée ici avec des pantalons légers vert, et un couvre-chef arabe. Les 'belt-kits' sont fabriquées par les soldats à partir d'articles britanniques et étrangers.

F1 Windproof et pantalons SAS en tissus de camouflage DPM; équipement pour parachutage de haute altitude—le sac à dos est poussé derrière les jambes. **F2** Les officiers portent le béret beige de préférence au casquette. **F3** Ceci est l'uniforme journalière pour tous les rangs.

G1 Porté rarement, cet uniforme est très semblable à celui de **D2**. Les officiers, à partir du rang de major, portaient ces pantalons overall étroits, modèle cavalerie. **G2** L'uniforme de parade est rarement porté par les troupes—les galons de modèle Rifles sont toujours portés par ce régiment. **G3** Sac à dos et fusil sont tous les deux rayés de peinture de camouflage.

H1 Les vêtements sont en DPM. L'arme représentée est la mitraillette Sterling à silencieux. **H2** L'uniforme de parade Vert Lovat est particulier aux Marines; le béret verts, aux commandos de Marines. Les insignes de métal sont noirs mat, et les insignes de rangs dorés. **H3** Les détails particuliers de l'équipement des unités anti-terroristes ne sont pas données; ceci est une approximation à partir de photographies. L'appareil respiratoire a sa radio intégrale. Des vêtements noirs non réfléchissants sont montrés ici, avec une veste anti-balle de modèle policier. L'arme est le H & K HP5A3. L'explosif de charpente est pour faire sauter les fenêtres.

Farbtafeln

A1 Eine Kombination von tropischer Kleidung nach Vorschrift und arabischen Gegenständen; der Einzelne hatte grosse Kleidungsfreiheit. SAS-Typ Fallschirmabzeichen auf der Brust. **A2** Vorgeschriebene Offiziers-Schirmmütze mit Regimentsabzeichen. Der Dufflecoat, Cordhosen und Wildlederschuhe weren populäre, wenn auch inoffizielle Kleidungsstücke in der Wüste. **A3** Die kurze Zeit benutzte weisse 'Chasseur Baskenmütze', getragen mit dem vorgeschriebenen battledress.

B1 SAS Abzeichen, an einer kastanienbraunen Baskenmütze der Airborne Forces getragen. Der mit Kapuze versehene Tarnungskittel wurde von einigem Personal getragen, andere erhielten den Denison Kittel der Fallschirmjäger. Hosen mit vergrösserter Oberschenkeltasche sind Airborne Forces-Ausgabe. **B2** Viel persönlicher Spielraum in der Kleidung und den Waffen war erlaubt; bemerke die bestimmte SAS Baskenmütze in hellbeige. **B3** Eine Mischung von britischen und französischen Abzeichen wird hier getragen.

C1 Britische tropische Uniform, einschliesslich der Baskenmütze 'type Gurka', und einer Mischung von US und britischem Gürtelzeug. Die grossen britischen Beutel wurden oft nach der Zuweisung von US-Ausrüstung zurückbehalten, da sie genau die Magazine für das FM 24/29 Maschinengewehr unterbringen konnten. **C2** Aus praktischen Gründen trug die australische SAS in Vietnam Kleidung und Ausrüstung der US Armee. **C3** Tarnungsuniform und Mütze von rhodesischer Herstellung.

D1 Die Uniforme dieses Reserve-Luftlandebataillons vereint traditionelle Abzeichenarten der Luftlandetruppen (kastanienbraune Baskenmütze); der Rifles (schwarze und grüne Rangwinkel); und der Artists' Rifles (das 'Mars und Minerva' Abzeichen), dem traditionellen Regiment, von dem es zusammengestellt wurde. **D2** Zeremonielle Uniform wurde für die Krönung von Königin Elisabeth eingeführt. **D3** Die beige Baskenmütze ersetzte schliesslich die kastanienbraune Baskenmütze im Jahre 1957. Üblicher Denison Kittel der Fallschirmjäger; das Gürtelzeug nach Regimenttradition geschwärzt. Die Waffen wurden in dem Packen unterhalb des Reservefallschirmpacks auf der Brust getragen.

E1 Tropische Uniform nach Vorschrift; Gürtelzeug nach dem Muster von 1944; US Karabiner M1; und bemerke das Djungelmesser der Eingeborenen, welches der Ausrüstung beigefügt ist. **E2** Weisse tropische Zeremonieuniform, noch zu diesem Zeitpunkt mit der kastanienbraunen Baskenmütze getragen; die Schärpe lässt den Unteroffizier vom Dienst erkennen. **E3** Der SAS Tarnungskittel mit Kapuze oder 'windproof' wird mit leichten grünen Hosen getragen, und ein arabisches Kopftuch. Gürtelausrüstung ist vom Einzelnen aus britischen und fremden Gegenständen zusammengestellt.

F1 SAS 'windproof' und Hosen aus DPM Tarnungsmaterial; Ausrüstung für das Fallschirmspringen aus grosser Höhe. Der Rucksack ist hinter den Beinen geschlungen. **F2** Die Offiziere tragen die beige Baskenmütze lieber als die Schirmmütze. **F3** Dies ist die normale Alltagsuniform aller Dienstgrade.

G1 Selten getragen, diese Uniform ist der von D2 sehr ähnlich. Offiziere vom Rang des Majors aufwärts tragen diese engen 'overall' Hosen nach Kavalleriemuster. **G2** Die Paradeuniform der Truppen wird selten getragen. Winkel nach dem Muster der Rifles werden noch von diesem Regiment getragen. **G3** Rucksack und Gewehr sind beide mit Tarnungsfarbe gestreift überzogen.

H1 Die Kleidung ist im DPM Tarnungsmuster; die Waffe ist die schallgedämpfte Sterling Maschinenpistole. **H2** Die 'Lovat' grüne Paradeuniform ist eine Eigenart der Royal Marines; die grüne Baskenmütze die der Marine Commandos. Metallabzeichen sind mattschwarz und Rangabzeichen golden. **H3** Einzelheiten der Ausrüstung der anti-Terroristen Einheiten werden noch nicht bekanntgegeben; diese Annäherung ist von Fotografien. Die Gasmaske hat ein Radio installiert. Schwarze nicht reflektierende Kleidung ist getragen, mit einer kugelsicheren Jacke nach Polizeimuster. Die Waffe ist die H & K HP5A3. Die 'rahmenförmige Sprengladung' ist da, um Fenster einzudrücken.